Henry Kett

History the Interpreter of Prophecy

Or, a view of Scriptural prophecies and their accomplishment in the past and present occurrences of the world: with conjectures respecting their future completion. Vol. 2

Henry Kett

History the Interpreter of Prophecy
Or, a view of Scriptural prophecies and their accomplishment in the past and present occurrences of the world: with conjectures respecting their future completion. Vol. 2

ISBN/EAN: 9783337308315

Printed in Europe, USA, Canada, Australia, Japan

Cover: Foto ©ninafisch / pixelio.de

More available books at **www.hansebooks.com**

HISTORY

THE

INTERPRETER OF PROPHECY,

OR,

A VIEW

OF

SCRIPTURAL PROPHECIES

AND

THEIR ACCOMPLISHMENT

IN THE

PAST AND PRESENT

OCCURRENCES OF THE WORLD;

WITH

CONJECTURES RESPECTING THEIR FUTURE
COMPLETION.

BY HENRY KETT, B.D.

FELLOW OF TRINITY COLLEGE, OXFORD, AND ONE
OF HIS MAJESTY'S PREACHERS AT WHITEHALL.

IN THREE VOLUMES.

VOL. II.

OXFORD;

Printed for Meffrs. HANWELL and PARKER; and J. COOKE;
And fold by C. and J. RIVINGTON, St. Paul's Church-Yard;
ROBSON, Bond-Street; EGERTON, Whitehall;
CADELL and DAVIES, Strand; and HAT-
CHARD, Piccadilly, London.
MDCCXCIX.

ADVERTISEMENT

TO

VOL. II.

———

THIS Work has been delayed and increased much beyond the original design, stated in the Introductory Chapter to the first Volume. This delay and this increase are to be attributed to my anxiety to obtain from the same Pen, to which I am indebted for so much assistance in the first Volume, A DEVELOPEMENT OF THE PROPHETICAL SCHEME CONCERNING ANTICHRIST; being well convinced, that no one could present this new and comprehensive system to the public in so clear a light, as the person with whom the ideas originated.

nated. To this Perfon I am obliged for the whole of the following Preliminary Chapter, except only the Hiftorical proofs of the early opinions, concerning the Papal Antichrift—and for nearly the whole of the third Volume.

CONTENTS

OF

VOL. II.

CLASS II.

PROPHECIES RELATING TO THE REIGN OF ANTICHRIST, AND THE REIGN AND FINAL TRIUMPH OF THE MESSIAH.

INTRODUCTORY CHAPTER.

Statement of the grounds for the Opinion, that the PAPAL, *the* MAHOMETAN, *and the* INFIDEL POWERS, *are different branches or forms of* THE SAME ANTICHRISTIAN POWER—*and that* ALL *are expresly foretold in Scripture, as permitted to arise in different ages of the world, for the purposes of punishment and trial to the Church of Christ.*

Pro-

CONTENTS.

Prophecies respecting ANTICHRIST, p. 1.
Proposed APPLICATION *of the above Prophecies,* p. 24.
Objections obviated, p. 28.
The PAPAL POWER *one Branch or Form of Antichrist,* p. 36.
The MAHOMETAN POWER *another Branch or Form of Antichrist,* p. 44.
General View of the Prophecies of Daniel. First Vision.—The IMAGE, p. 48.
Second Vision.—The FOUR BEASTS, *and the* LITTLE HORN *of Antichrist,* p. 57.
Third Vision—The RAM *and the* HE-GOAT, *including "the* LITTLE HORN" *of the East,* p. 66.
Fourth Vision.—"The KING" *of the West,* p. 89.
The INFIDEL POWER *a third Branch or Form of Antichrist shewn to be predicted by Daniel,* p. 107.
The general Opinion concerning the SECOND BEAST *in the Revelation of St. John, considered to be erroneous,* p. 116.

The

The INFIDEL POWER of *Antichrift fhewn to be predicted alfo in the Revelation*,
       p. 127.
CONCLUSION,   p. 161.

CHAPTER THE FIRST.

The Rife, Progrefs, Eftablifhment, and Decline of the PAPAL POWER OF ANTICHRIST—*or,* "THE KING OF THE WEST," *in the Vifions of Daniel, and* "THE FIRST BEAST" *in the Revelation of St. John,* p. 171—254.

CHAPTER THE SECOND.

The Rife, Progrefs, Eftablifhment, and Decline of the MAHOMETAN POWER OF ANTICHRIST—*or,* "THE LITTLE HORN OF THE EAST" *in the Vifions of Daniel; and* "THE LOCUSTS," *and* "THE EUPHRATEAN HORSEMEN," *under their* "KING APOLLYON," *in the Revelation of St. John,* p. 255—231.

CLASS II.

INTRODUCTORY CHAPTER.

THE moſt careleſs reader of the Prophetical parts of the Old and New Teſtament can ſcarcely fail to notice, that there are ſeveral ſtrong intimations, and many direct and clear predictions concerning a Power, a Perſon, or a ſucceſſion of Perſons, that were to ariſe in the world, and either deceitfully arrogate to themſelves the place and office of Chriſt, or maintain a direct enmity and oppoſition to Him and his Religion.—Such is the "ANTICHRIST," or "the many ANTICHRISTS," ſpoken of in the New Teſtament.

tament[a]. The characters and properties of thefe powers or perfons, the dignity which they were to affume, the means by which they were to recommend themfelves to the world, the arts which they were to practife, and the perfecution they were to carry on, to opprefs the true Chriftians, and obtain adherents to their errors, are all clearly reprefented in various paffages of Scripture.

[a] It may perhaps be neceffary to apprize the unlearned Reader, that the term *Antichrift* ('Αντίχριστος) is an epithet *generally* meaning any power or perfons acting in any refpect in oppofition to Chrift or his doctrines. Its *particular* meaning is to be collected from thofe paffages of Scripture, in which it occurs. " It may either fignify one who affumes the place and office of Chrift, or one who maintains a direct enmity and oppofition to him." See Hurd's Introduction to the Study of the Prophecies, vol. ii. p. 10.

Prophe-

Prophecies respecting ANTICHRIST.

In order to throw as much light as possible upon this subject, I shall collect the principal of these Prophecies into one point of view, before I venture to offer any observations upon them, excepting only the Prophecies of Daniel. These, as they will be stated particularly in the course of this Chapter, I shall omit here, to avoid a length of repetition; observing only that Daniel expresly mentions a power which was to arise from the *last* of the four great empires of the world, but was to be *divers from it*.

St. Paul, guided by the same spirit of Prophecy, directs the attention of the early Christian converts to a similar subject.

Now[b] *we beseech you, brethren, by the coming of our Lord Jesus Christ, and by our*

[b] 2 Thess. ii. 1—10.

gather-

gathering together unto him, that ye be not soon shaken in mind, or be troubled, neither by spirit, nor by word, nor by letter, as from us, as that the day of Christ is at hand. Let no man deceive you by any means. For that day shall not come, except there come a falling away first, and that man of sin be revealed, the son of perdition, who opposeth and exalteth himself above all that is called God, or that is worshipped: so that he as God sitteth in the temple of God, shewing himself that he is God. Remember ye not that when I was yet with you, I told you these things? And now ye know what withholdeth, that he might be revealed in his time. For the mystery of iniquity doth already work; only he who now letteth, will let until he be taken out of the way. And then shall that Wicked be revealed, whom the Lord shall consume with the spirit of his mouth, and shall destroy with the brightness of his coming: even him whose coming is after the working of Satan, with all power, and signs, and lying wonders, and with all deceivableness of

unrigh-

unrighteousness in them that perish; because they received not the love of the truth, that they might be saved.

The Apostle resumes the same subject in his first Epistle to Timothy, and forewarns him of some great apostasy, that was at some future time to happen; and he characterizes this great event by such peculiar and striking circumstances, as may lead *us*, who live in these *later* ages, at once to discover the particular persons to whom the description is applicable.

Now[c] *the spirit speaketh expressly, that in the latter times some shall depart from the faith, giving heed to seducing spirits, and doctrines of devils; speaking lies in hypocrisy, having their conscience seared with a hot iron; forbidding to marry, and commanding to abstain from meats, which God*

[c] 1 Tim. iv. 1, 2, 3.

hath

hath created to be received with thankfgiving of them which believe and know the truth.

^d*This know also, that in the last days perilous times shall come. For men shall be lovers of their own selves, covetous, boasters, proud, blasphemers, disobedient to parents, unthankful, unholy, without natural affection, truce-breakers, false accusers, incontinent, fierce, despisers of those that are good, traitors, heady, high-minded, lovers of pleasures more than lovers of God; having a form of godliness, but denying the power thereof. From such turn away.*

Ever learning, and never able to come to the knowledge of the truth. Now as Jannes and Jambres withstood Moses, so do these also resist truth; men of corrupt minds, reprobate concerning the faith. But they shall proceed no further; for their folly shall

---

[d] 2 Tim. iii. 1—5. 7, 8, 9, 13. iv. 3, 4.

be manifeſt unto all men, as theirs alſo was. But evil men and ſeducers ſhall wax worſe and worſe, deceiving and being deceived.

For the time will come when they will not endure ſound doctrine, but after their own luſt ſhall they heap to themſelves teachers, having itching ears; and they ſhall turn away their ears from the truth, and ſhall be turned unto fables.

A Power, ſimilar to that deſcribed by St. Paul, is likewiſe predicted by St. John.

ᵉ Little children, it is the laſt time; and as ye have heard that Antichriſt ſhall come, even now are there many Antichriſts; whereby we know that it is the laſt time. They went out from us, but they were not of us: for if they had been of us, they would no doubt have continued with us; but they

ᵉ 1 John ii. 18, 19, 22. iv. 3.

went out, that they might be made manifest that they were not all of us. Who is a liar, but he that denieth that Jesus is the Christ? He is Antichrist that denieth the Father and the Son.

And every spirit that confesseth not that Jesus Christ is come in the flesh, is not of God; and this is that spirit of Antichrist, whereof ye have heard that it should come, and even now already is it in the world.

But of such a Power a more full description is given in the Revelations, under the symbols of a horrible animal, which is represented rising from a stormy ocean, and becoming the object of astonishment to all who beheld it;—and of a creature which rising afterwards out of the earth, became equally formidable.

ˢ *And I stood upon the sand of the sea, and saw a beast rise up out of the sea, hav-*

―――――
ˢ Rev. xiii. 1—18.

ing

ing seven heads and ten horns, and upon his horns ten crowns, and upon his heads the name of blasphemy. And the beast which I saw was like unto a leopard, and his feet were as the feet of a bear, and his mouth as the mouth of a lion: and the dragon gave him his power, and his seat, and great authority. And I saw one of his heads as it were wounded to death; and his deadly wound was healed: and all the world wondered after the beast. And they worshipped the dragon, which gave power unto the beast: and they worshipped the beast, saying, Who is like unto the beast? Who is able to make war with him? And there was given unto him, a mouth speaking great things and blasphemies; and power was given unto him to continue forty and two months. And he opened his mouth in blasphemy against God, to blaspheme his name and his tabernacle, and them that dwell in heaven. And it was given unto him to make war with the saints, and to overcome them: and power was given him

over all kindreds, and tongues, and nations. And all that dwell upon the earth shall worship him, whose names are not written in the book of life, of the Lamb slain from the foundation of the world. If any man have an ear, let him hear. He that leadeth into captivity shall go into captivity: he that killeth with the sword must be killed with the sword. Here is the patience and the faith of the saints. And I beheld another beast coming up out of the earth, and he had two horns like a lamb, and he spake as a dragon. And he exerciseth all the power of the first beast before him, and causeth the earth and them which dwell therein to worship the first beast, whose deadly wound was healed. And he doeth great wonders, so that he maketh fire come down from heaven on the earth, in the sight of men, and deceiveth them that dwell on the earth by the means of those miracles which he had power to do in the sight of the beast; saying to them that dwell on the earth, That they should make an image to
the

the beaſt which had the wound by a ſword, and did live. And he had power to give life unto the image of the beaſt, that the image of the beaſt ſhould both ſpeak, and cauſe that as many as would not worſhip the image of the beaſt, ſhould be killed. And he cauſed all both ſmall and great, rich and poor, free and bond, to receive a mark in their right hand, or in their foreheads; and that no man might buy or ſell, ſave he that had the mark, or the name of the beaſt, or the number of his name. Here is wiſdom. Let him that hath underſtanding count the number of the beaſt : for it is the number of a man ; and his number is ſix hundred threeſcore and ſix.

And St. John afterwards foretels its downfall.

^{g} And after theſe things I ſaw another angel come down from heaven, having great

^{g} Rev. xviii. 1—8.

power; and the earth was lightened with his glory. And he cried mightily with a strong voice, saying, Babylon the great is fallen, is fallen, and is become the habitation of devils, and the hold of every foul spirit, and a cage of every unclean and hateful bird. For all nations have drunk of the wine of the wrath of her fornication, and the kings of the earth have committed fornication with her, and the merchants of the earth are waxed rich through the abundance of her delicacies. And I heard another voice from heaven, saying, Come out of her, my people, that ye be not partakers of her sins, and that ye receive not of her plagues. For her sins have reached unto heaven, and God hath remembered her iniquities. Reward her even as she rewarded you, and double unto her double according to her works: in the cup which she hath filled fill to her double. How much she hath glorified herself, and lived deliciously, so much torment and sorrow give her. For she saith in her heart, I sit a queen, and am no widow,

widow, and shall see no sorrow. Therefore shall her plagues come in one day, death, and mourning, and famine; and she shall be utterly burned with fire; for strong is the Lord God who judgeth her.

Another great Power is likewise predicted: the description of it is marked with many striking symbols, and characteristics, and its progress and destructive ravages are clearly pointed out.

[h] *And the fifth angel sounded, and I saw a star fall from heaven unto the earth; and to him was given the key of the bottomless pit. And he opened the bottomless pit; and there arose a smoke out of the pit, as the smoke of a great furnace: and the sun and the air were darkened by reason of the smoke of the pit. And there came out of the smoke locusts upon the earth; and unto them was given power, as the scorpions of the earth*

[h] Rev. ix. 1—21.

have power. And it was commanded them that they should not hurt the grass of the earth, neither any green thing, neither any tree; but only those men which have not the seal of God in their foreheads. And to them it was given that they should not kill them, but that they should be tormented five months; and their torment was as the torment of a scorpion, when he striketh a man. And in those days shall men seek death, and shall not find it; and shall desire to die, and death shall flee from them. And the shapes of the locusts were like unto horses prepared unto battle; and on their heads were as it were crowns like gold, and their faces were as the faces of men. And they had hair as the hair of women, and their teeth were as the teeth of lions. And they had breast-plates as it were breast-plates of iron; and the sound of their wings was as the sound of chariots, of many horses running to battle. And they had tails like unto scorpions, and there were stings in their tails; and their power was to hurt men five months. And they

they had a king over them, which is the angel of the bottomless pit, whose name in the Hebrew tongue is Abaddon, but in the Greek tongue hath his name Apollyon. One wo is past; and behold there come two woes more hereafter. And the sixth angel sounded, and I heard a voice from the four horns of the golden altar which is before God, saying to the sixth angel which had the trumpet, Loose the four angels, which are bound in the great river Euphrates. And the four angels were loosed, which were prepared for an hour, and a day, and a month, and a year, for to slay the third part of men. And the number of the army of the horsemen were two hundred thousand thousand; and I heard the number of them. And thus I saw the horses in the vision, and them that sat on them, having breast-plates of fire, and of jacinth, and brimstone; and the heads of the horses were as the heads of lions; and out of their mouths issued fire, and smoke, and brimstone. By these three was the third part of men killed, by the
fire,

fire, and by the smoke, and by the brimstone, which issued out of their mouths. For their power is in their mouth, and in their tails; for their tails were like unto serpents, and had heads, and with them they do hurt. And the rest of the men which were not killed by these plagues, yet repented not of the works of their hands, that they should not worship devils, and idols of gold, and silver, and brass, and stone, and of wood, which neither can see, nor hear, nor walk: neither repented they of their murders, nor of their sorceries, nor of their fornication, nor of their thefts.

St. Peter and St. Jude expressly speak of a great apostasy from the Christian faith, when false teachers should tempt Christians to the greatest dissoluteness of conduct, and poison their minds with Infidelity.

[i] *But there were false Prophets also among*

---

[i] 2 Pet. ii, iii.

the

the people, even as there shall be false teachers among you, who privily shall bring in damnable heresies, even denying the Lord that bought them, and bring upon themselves swift destruction. And many shall follow their pernicious ways, by reason of whom the way of truth shall be evil spoken of. And through covetousness shall they with feigned words make merchandize of you; whose judgment now of a long time lingereth not, and their damnation slumbereth not. For if God spared not the angels that sinned, but cast them down to hell, and delivered them into chains of darkness, to be reserved unto judgment; and spared not the old world, but saved Noah the eighth person, a preacher of righteousness, bringing in the flood upon the world of the ungodly; and turning the cities of Sodom and Gomorrah into ashes, condemned them with an overthrow, making them an ensample unto those that after should live ungodly; and delivered just Lot, vexed with the filthy conversation of the wicked: (for that righteous

teous man dwelling among them, in seeing and hearing vexed his righteous soul from day to day with their unlawful deeds.) The Lord knoweth how to deliver the godly out of temptations, and to reserve the unjust unto the day of judgment to be punished. But chiefly them that walk after the flesh in the lust of uncleanness, and despise government; presumptuous are they, self-willed, they are not afraid to speak evil of dignities: whereas angels, which are greater in power and might, bring not railing accusation against them before the Lord. But these, as natural brute beasts made to be taken and destroyed, speak evil of the things that they understand not, and shall utterly perish in their own corruption; and shall receive the reward of unrighteousness, as they that count it pleasure to riot in the day time; spots they are and blemishes, sporting themselves with their own deceivings, while they feast with you; having eyes full of adultery, and that cannot cease from sin; beguiling unstable souls; an heart they have exercised with covetous

prac-

practices; cursed children; which have forsaken the right way, and are gone astray, following the way of Balaam the son of Bosor, who loved the wages of unrighteousness; but was rebuked for his iniquity; the dumb ass speaking with man's voice, forbad the madness of the Prophet. These are wells without water, clouds that are carried with a tempest; to whom the mist of darkness is reserved for ever. For when they speak great swelling words of vanity, they allure through the lusts of the flesh, through much wantonness, those that were clean escaped from them who live in error. While they promise them liberty, they themselves are the servants of corruption; for of whom a man is overcome, of the same is he brought in bondage. For if after they have escaped the pollutions of the world, through the knowledge of the Lord and Saviour Jesus Christ, they are again entangled therein, and overcome, the latter end is worse with them than the beginning. For it had been better for them not to have known the way of righteousness, teoufnefs, than, after they have known it, to turn from the holy commandment delivered unto them. But it is happened unto them according to the true proverb, *The dog is turned to his own vomit again*; *and the fow that was wafhed, to her wallowing in the mire.* This fecond Epiftle, beloved, I now write unto you; in both which I ftir up your pure minds by way of remembrance; that ye may be mindful of the words which were fpoken before by the holy Prophets, and of the commandment of us the Apoftles of the Lord and Saviour. Knowing this firft, that there fhall come in the laft days fcoffers, walking after their own lufts, and faying, Where is the promife of his coming? for fince the fathers fell afleep, all things continue as they were from the beginning of the creation. For this they willingly are ignorant of, that by the word of God the heavens were of old, and the earth ftanding out of the water, and in the water; whereby the world that then was, being overflowed with water, perifhed. But the heavens

vens and the earth, which are now, by the same word are kept in store, reserved unto fire against the day of judgment and perdition of ungodly men. But, beloved, be not ignorant of this one thing, that one day is with the Lord as a thousand years, and a thousand years as one day. The Lord is not slack concerning his promise, as some men count slackness; but is long suffering to usward, not willing that any should perish, but that all should come to repentance. But the day of the Lord will come as a thief in the night, in the which the heavens shall pass away with a great noise, and the elements shall melt with fervent heat, the earth also and the works that are therein shall be burnt up. Seeing then that all these things shall be dissolved, what manner of persons ought ye to be in all holy conversation and godliness; looking for, and hasting unto the coming of the day of God; wherein the heavens being on fire shall be dissolved, and the elements shall melt with fervent heat. Nevertheless we, according to his promise,
look

look for new heavens and a new earth, wherein dwelleth righteousness. Wherefore, beloved, seeing that ye look for such things, be diligent, that ye may be found of him in peace, without spot and blameless. And account that the long suffering of our Lord is salvation; even as our beloved brother Paul also, according to the wisdom given unto him, hath written unto you; as also in all his Epistles, speaking in them of these things; in which are some things hard to be understood, which they that are unlearned and unstable wrest, as they do also the other Scriptures, unto their own destruction. Ye therefore, beloved, seeing ye know these things before, beware lest ye also, being led away with the error of the wicked, fall from your own stedfastness. But grow in grace, and in the knowledge of our Lord and Saviour Jesus Christ. To him be glory both now and for ever. Amen.

[k] *For there are certain men crept in unawares,*

---

[k] Jude 4, 8, 16, 17, 18, 19.

wares, who were before of old ordained to this condemnation; ungodly men, turning the grace of our God into lasciviousness, and denying the only Lord God, and our Lord Jesus Christ. Likewise also these filthy dreamers defile the flesh, despise dominion, and speak evil of dignities. These are murmurers, complainers, walking after their own lusts; and their mouth speaketh great swelling words, having men's persons in admiration because of advantage. But, beloved, remember ye the words which were spoken before of the Apostles of our Lord Jesus Christ; how that they told you there should be mockers in the last time, who should walk after their own ungodly lusts. These be they, who separate themselves, sensual, having not the Spirit.

Propofed APPLICATION *of the above Prophecies.*

From all thefe defcriptions taken together, it clearly appears that A POWER, fometimes reprefented as the *little horn*, the *man of fin*, the *Antichrift*, the *beaft*, the *harlot*, the *ftar fallen from heaven*, the *falfe Prophet*, the *dragon*, or as the operation of *falfe teachers*, was to be expected to arife in the Chriftian world, to perfecute, opprefs, and delude the Difciples of Chrift, corrupt the doctrines of the primitive church, enact new laws, and eftablifh its dominion over the minds of mankind.

Such are the names, the characteriftics, and the qualities of this power of Antichrift, which I confider to be THE POWER OF THE DRAGON himfelf—explained by the angel, to be that old ferpent which

which is the Devil or Satan[1]—the old enemy of mankind, beginning and ending his rebellious war with *deceit* and *lies*.—Cast from his throne of *Pagan* Rome when Christianity was established in the seat of empire, and the triumphant church enjoyed a short repose, he returned *secretly* to the contest, and disturbed its peace by heresies and consequent animosities, corrupted it through the medium of prosperity, and reduced it, excepting only a very small part, to a state requiring correction and punishment for having yielded to temptations which obedience to the laws of its divine Master would have enabled it to resist.—Then was the Dragon again permitted to exalt himself to the throne of this world—But in the same manner as the captivity of the Jews was *previously* limited to the term of 70 years, to prove it the punishment allotted by God, and

---

[1] Rev. xx. 2.

not the *conquest of the heathen* over his people; so the *reign* of the Dragon or Antichrist, was *previously* limited[m] to 1260 years, to prove that the sufferings of the church are by the appointment of God, and *not* the *triumph of the Dragon* over the church of Christ.—Babylon was destroyed at the expiration of the 70 years; and when the 1260 years shall be expired, "the Dragon......shall be bound and cast into the bottomless pit[n]."

If we follow the course of history as connected with Christianity, we first discover the existence of this Power in a general sense in the age of St. John, when the Gnostic and other heresies began to arise; for it is acknowledged many of these Prophecies allude to the different *heresies* that *have* troubled, and

[m] See Daniel vii. 25. Rev. xi. 3. Pyle on the Revelations, p. 80.
[n] Rev. xx. 2.

do

do trouble the church. These however are of a fluctuating nature; they rise, spread, decline, increase again, or die away when "their folly becomes manifest to all." But there appear to be three great *forms* of Antichrist, which were to *continue stedfastly* in *great power*, and assume much more alarming appearances of corruption, persecution, and hostility; and it is to these we now direct our attention.

It will be the object of the three following Chapters to shew, from the application of Prophecy to History, and to the remarkable train of events which are *now* passing in the world, how exactly POPERY, MAHOMETANISM, and INFIDELITY correspond with the characters given in Scripture of the POWER of ANTICHRIST, which was to prevail a certain time for the especial trial and punishment of the corrupted church of Christ.

Objections obviated.

But considering the strenuous efforts which are now made to undermine the credit of Prophecy, by the continual cry of *vague language, uncertain meaning, and contradictory assertions,* uttered by artifice, and echoed by ignorance,—I shall first endeavour to prove, not only that the Prophecies themselves are clear, determinate, and harmonious, but that the different interpretations of the learned men, who have written upon this subject, will be found consistent with each other upon those points which were fairly open to their observation—and that the difference in their opinions arises from the different views they took of *the same Power*, without having sufficiently considered that this power was to appear in various forms in different ages of the world.—To this end it will be

un-

unneceffary to mention the very numerous circumftances concerning which they agree; and thefe are indeed, in general, the moft important points of thofe Prophecies which they faw to have been fulfilled—the points in which they differ are chiefly thofe which the events of *later times* appear to render capable of a *clearer explanation*. And to thefe points will the following fhort account of the opinions of the principal Commentators be confined, with a view to remove fome of the difficulties, and reconcile fome of the different interpretations to one point of reference; and this, it is prefumed, will throw confiderable light upon thofe parts of the prophetical writings which have been moft violently attacked, and therefore will materially ferve the great caufe, which it is the object of this work to fupport.

It is important to obferve, that if the Prophecies of the Old Teftament are allowed

lowed to admit of a firft and alfo a fecondary accomplifhment, there appears to be no reafon why a fimilar mode of interpretation fhould not be adopted refpecting the Prophecies of the New Teftament. Yet this point has fcarcely ever been attended to.—Proteftants, fuffering under the power of the Papacy, or infenfibly led by their religious opinions, have feen the *whole* of Antichrift in the Church of Rome, or fome power or powers connected with it.—They faw the Prophecy to be in many parts *clearly* applicable to the Church of Rome, and they looked for no other accomplifhment; though the difficulty, with which many paffages are brought to apply to this object, indicates it to be but a primary or partial fulfilment; and this difficulty led to differences of opinion, which, to the eye of fuperficial readers, appears to have thrown an obfcurity over the whole fubject. It is clear however from the Prophecies themfelves, that a long feries of of time is required for their fulfilment; and though it is *defigned* that we fhould fee *as much* of the Prophecies fulfilling *in our own times* as to *guard* us againft the evils and dangers prevalent in thofe times, we fhould be cautious in *reftricting* the fenfe of any to one particular period, excepting thofe which are evidently thus confined by Scripture. If it be obvioufly abfurd to imagine we can judge with certainty refpecting the *time* and *manner* in which events plainly predicted will be accomplifhed in future, it is equally fo to imagine that our anceftors could judge of the prefent times as clearly as we can do. Some portion of novelty therefore in an interpretation can be no objection to its truth, provided it harmonizes with eftablifhed opinion concerning the principal points of Prophecy itfelf.

"It is a part of this Prophecy" (fays Sir I. Newton in his Obfervations on the

the Apocalypfe, which he confiders as fo clofely connected with the Prophecies of Daniel, as " making together but one complete Prophecy") " that it fhould not be" (fully) " underftood before the laft age of the world; and therefore it makes for the credit of the Prophecy, that it is not yet underftood. But if the laft age—the age of opening thefe things—be now approaching, as by the great fucceffes of late interpreters it feems to be, we have more encouragement than ever to look into thefe things."......" Amongft the interpreters of the laft age there is fcarce one of note, who hath not made *fome difcovery* worth knowing; and thence I feem to gather that God is about opening thefe myfteries."

Thefe fcattered lights thrown upon different parts of the fubject muft greatly affift other Commentators in the progrefs of their *later* refearches; and we may

may surely indulge the hope, that the *increasing* clearness of this Prophecy, will operate with *increasing* power, as the time of its fulfilment draws nearer. " And the remnant were affrighted, and gave glory to God," *previous* to the seventh trumpet, which is to " finish these mysteries of God."

We may farther observe, that the difference of opinion among Commentators upon *particular parts* of a Prophecy, does not invalidate their testimony as a proof of the truth of those *great points*, in which they agree; or even the *precision* of the Prophecy itself in *all* its parts, though that precision cannot be seen by us till the course of events presents it to our view.—For example, *all* agree that the corruption and distress of the church in the latter ages of the world, and the final triumph of our Lord over all his enemies, have been clearly foretold in the Old and in the

New Testament. But whether the reign of Antichrist be the establishment of the Papal power, or of Mahometanism, or of Infidelity and Atheism, or of all united, may be disputed till *events determine* the question; according as the different writers are influenced by situation, course of study, turn of mind, and attention to passing circumstances, or now *perhaps*, by political principles; for in no times was *caution* in interpretation ever more necessary than in these, when *Party Spirit* in religion and in politics is so prevalent as to mingle itself almost imperceptibly " with the thoughts of almost every man's heart." If, however, the *present* are times of greater *general* distress and alarm than history can furnish any account of—if the *series* of Prophecies and their corresponding events that are *past* and *generally acknowledged* to be *understood*, is brought down near enough to our own times to mark *whereabouts* we are in the *series of trumpets and vials*—it will

will be surely difficult to deny that "the Antichrist *is* come," and that "the judgments of God are" *now* "abroad in the earth," though the *appropriation* of the title of Antichrist to any particular power, or united powers, be left undecided. "* If indeed it be true, as the Romanists pretend, that this part of the Prophecy is not yet fulfilled, and that *Antichrist will come only for a little time, before the general judgment*, it would be in vain to enquire who, or what he is; we should split upon the same rock as the Fathers have done; it would better become us to say with Calmet, that, "*as the reign of Antichrist is still remote*, we cannot shew the accomplishment of the Prophecies with regard to him:" but if the system which I presume to offer concerning *the power of Antichrist* be right, it will appear that these different opinions of the Protestants and Papists, derived from *partial* views of the subject, are not wholly incompatible with each other.

* Newton, vol. i. p. 476.

The PAPAL POWER *one Branch or Form of Antichrist.*

With respect to the commonly received opinion, that the Church of Rome is Antichrist, the Divines of the Church of England, as well as most of the Divines of the Protestant churches abroad, who have written upon the subject, concur in maintaining, that these Prophecies of Daniel, of St. Paul, and St. John, that have been quoted, point directly to the Church of Rome. And the members of that Church cannot complain, that the application of these Prophecies has been made by men incompetent to the discussion of such a subject; for perhaps, in the whole compass of the learned world, it would be difficult to find those who possessed more candour, learning, diligence, acuteness, or zeal for the discovery of truth, than the writers who have turned their attention this way.

The

The subject has been examined and illustrated, and this important point has been determined by Mede and Newton, Daubuz and Clarke, Lowman and Hurd, Jurieu, Vitringa, and many other illustrious members of the Protestant Churches.

The first Reformers likewise, in the most strong and explicit terms, charged the See of Rome with her Antichristian spirit, and urged, in their own defence and vindication, the authority of those Prophetical warnings that encouraged all true Christians "to depart out of her communion, that they might not be partakers of her plagues." This was the constant exhortation of Wickliff, of Luther, and of Jewell; and such was the language of their followers. They were sensible of the value of the arguments drawn from these Prophecies in favour of their secession and separation from a corrupted and erroneous Church, and they

they failed not to oppofe them to their adverfaries with the greateft zeal and energy.

That their conduct was highly juftifiable, is clear from what we may collect from the moft authentic records of Ecclefiaftical Hiftory; becaufe we find that the very fame interpretation was given to thefe predictions, not only long before any controverfy was moved between the Papifts and the Proteftants, but before any fuch diftinctions of Chriftians were known to the world.

It was the reigning opinion of the Chriftians of the earlieft times, that Antichrift would appear foon after the fall of the Roman Empire. They looked forward to this event as fo replete with alarm and danger to the church, that it was a cuftom to introduce particular prayers in their liturgy for the continuance of the Empire of Pagan Rome; that

that the coming of Antichrift might be delayed. St. Jerom, who flourifhed in the fourth century, in his Commentary upon the Prophecies of Daniel, delivers the general opinion of his age in thefe remarkable words; " Let us affert, in conformity with the fentiments of all the Ecclefiaftical writers, that towards the end of the world, when the Roman Empire fhall be deftroyed, ten kings fhall come, and divide the Empire, and an eleventh king fhall arife, in whom Satan fhall dwell corporeally, who fhall fubdue three of thefe ten kings."

St. Cyril, who likewife flourifhed in the fourth century, afferted exprefsly, " that the eleventh king mentioned by Daniel, is Antichrift, who fhall violently feize, by magical and wicked contrivance, the Roman power."

In the fixth century, Gregory the Great, in the moft plain and direct manner,

ner, in his addresses to the most eminent persons of his own time, scrupled not to apply the Prophecies concerning the beast in the Revelations, the man of sin, and the apostacy from the faith, mentioned by St. Paul, to him who should presume to claim the title of Universal Priest, or Universal Bishop, in the Christian Church. "I affirm confidently," said he, "that whoever calls himself Universal Bishop, or is desirous to be so called, shows himself, by this pride and elation of heart, to be the forerunner of Antichrist." Such was his language, intended to convey a severe censure upon the Patriarch of Constantinople. Yet this zealous Bishop of Rome was blind to his own situation; for no one before his time had ever carried the claims and the arrogance of Papal supremacy to such a pitch, as himself: and it is remarkable, that his immediate successor, Boniface III.. received from the tyrant Phocas, the exact

act title which Gregory had thus censured.

At the Synod of Rheims, held in the tenth century, Arnulphus, Bishop of Orleans, appealed to the whole Council, whether the Bishop of Rome was not the Antichrist of the Prophets, " sitting in the temple of God," and perfectly corresponding with the marks which St. Paul had given of him.

In the eleventh century all the characters of Antichrist seemed to be so united in the person of Pope Hildebrand, who took the name of Gregory VII. that Joannes Aventinus, a Romish Historian, speaks of it as a subject in which the generality of fair, candid, and ingenuous writers, agreed that at that time began the reign of Antichrist.—St. Barnard, in the twelfth century, employed the force of his great eloquence against the corruptions of the See of Rome.

Rome. "The Popes," said he, "call themselves the ministers of Christ, and they serve Antichrist. The beast of the Revelations, to whom was given a mouth speaking blasphemies, and to war with the saints, seizes the chair of St. Peter, like a lion ready for his prey." And to close this detail, the Albigenses and Waldenses, who may be called the Protestants of the twelfth and thirteenth centuries, expressly asserted in their declarations of faith, that the Church of Rome was the whore of Babylon.

Thus have we a regular chain of testimony[p] to prove the successive progress of this opinion within the period alluded to, viz. from the time of the Apostles to the Reformation. In proportion as the authority of the Popes prevailed,

---

[p] All the parts of this chain are clearly shown in the learned and ingenious Introduction of Bishop Hurd to the Study of the Prophecies; from whence I have chiefly selected the above detail.

and extinguished freedom of inquiry, these explanations of the Prophecies were checked, except in the case of some few persons, who had boldness enough to assert them publicly, in defiance of the decrees of the Conclave, that menaced them with excommunication. The application therefore of these Prophecies to Papal Rome, far from being a *novel opinion*, published to vindicate the conduct of the Reformers and their adherents, was authorized by *an antient* and *uninterrupted tradition* in the Church, grounded upon *Prophecy*, and the *words* of the *Apostles*, and was fully justified by the *declarations*, *conduct*, and *institutions of the Papists themselves*, when exercising their oppressive authority over the Christian world [q].

The

[q] It is curious to inquire whether the Papists behold in this prophetical picture any likeness of themselves. They imagine they view in it imperial Rome elated by her victories, exulting in her

The MAHOMETAN POWER *another Branch, or Form of Antichrist.*

All Commentators agree that the ninth chapter of Revelations refers to

her senfuality, and her spoils; polluted by idolatry, persecuting the people of God, and finally falling like the first Babylon: whilst a new and holy city, represented by their own communion, filled with the spotless votaries of the Christian faith, rises out of its ruins, and the victory of the cross is completed over the temples of Paganism. This scheme has its able advocates, at the head of whom may be placed Bossuet, the pious and learned Bishop of Meaux, the enlightened and candid Grotius, and the acute and diligent Hammond. They have indeed discovered a faint and imperfect resemblance; but have they pointed out the particular nice and distinct traces of likeness? The greatest difficulties stand in the way of their system, which all their learning and ingenuity cannot remove. For, in order to establish their point, they run into a palpable absurdity, by violating the order of time, disregarding the opinions of the primitive Christians, and turning away their eyes from the appropriate descriptions of the Prophets.

Mahometanism, and the Saracenic and Turkish powers. It is therefore clear, that the present generation is still living under the influence of the sixth trumpet, when the *four angels* [that is, the four Turkish Sultanies] *were loosed, which were bound in the great river Euphrates*. The time for their conquest was exactly limited, and history ascertains that this time was not exceeded; but *nothing* is said in this chapter of the *duration* of their dominion. However, since it is declared, that " in the days of the voice of the seventh angel, the mystery of God shall be finished," it is *certain* that this dominion must be destroyed towards the end of the sixth trumpet, or "when the seventh shall *begin* to sound."

Thus far is *clear.*—What follows I would be understood to offer as *conjecture* only; but I dare not offer even a conjecture relative to Prophecies which
are

are not yet fulfilled, without stating the grounds upon which it is founded.—It is very generally allowed that the six vials are poured out during the sixth trumpet, and that the seventh trumpet and seventh vial are contemporary.—The sixth vial is poured out upon the great river Euphrates; and the water thereof is dried up, that the way of the kings of the East may be prepared." Considering the Turkish power as originating in the Euphrates (if I may so speak), and that this river runs through the Asiatic part of their empire, I suppose the seat of the Asiatic Antichrist—the Turkish Empire will either suffer very considerable diminution, or be entirely removed, under the sixth vial.—This opinion does not imply the *destruction* of Mahometanism, any more than the fifth vial implies the *destruction* of Popery—but I think *both* the fifth and sixth vials will produce the decay and downfal of the *power* of both, though both will continue to *exist* " till the

the time of the end." It should be observed, that " the way for the kings of the East '" is " only *prepared*" by this vial; they do not even appear, nor is there any thing more said of them under that title—The explanation and the consummation of the " mystery" is reserved for the seventh trumpet—nothing even *seems* to conclude till then. The seven vials *are poured out in succession*; but it does not follow that one *ends* when another *begins*; on the contrary, I think it *highly probable* that the first will *continue* to the seventh. We find that the *first* of the seven vials was poured out

---

' Various have been the conjectures concerning these " Kings of the East:" some believe them to be the Eastern nations—some the *ten* tribes of Israel concealed in Tartary, or India—some the Jews, or the twelve tribes collectively from the whole world—some, the restoration of the Christian religion in its antient churches.—It is not perhaps impossible to reconcile most of these opinions with each other.

upon the men " which had the mark of the beaft, and upon them (alfo) which worfhipped his image."—In fhort, after confidering the *contents* of the *vials*, and comparing them with hiftory and the prefent ftate of the world, I think it appears that the feventh vial will find all the fix former vials *plaguing* the earth—the firft having had the *longeft* and the fixth the *fhorteft* run. According to this mode of interpretation, Antichrift in all its forms—Heretical, Papal, Mahometan, and Infidel—will be upon the ftage in the *laft* fcene of this great drama, and will *all* have their place in the final cataftrophe.

General View of the Prophecies of Daniel. Firft Vifion.—*The* IMAGE.

Before I proceed to ftate the grounds upon which I have ventured to found the

the opinion, that Infidelity is the third branch or form of the predicted Antichrist, I muft requeft the Reader to take a general view of the Prophecies of Daniel, which will indeed lay before him a complete view of the whole fubject, and afford additional evidence to the harmony of the prophetic fcheme.

The diffidence natural to a mind ftrongly impreffed with the importance and facred nature of the fubject it is about to difcufs, renders me anxious to conduct the Reader by a regular train of eftablifhed interpretation and accomplifhment, to the great points which form a material part of my hypothefis; and I truft it will be allowed, that the following fhort account of the Prophecies concerning the four great empires, places the *different origin* of the powers which I apprehend to be *diftinct* from each other, in a confpicuous light. Upon a matter of fuch high importance the ferious

ferious inquirer after truth will value caution more than brevity.

" The golden head of the image'"' which Nebuchadnezzar faw in his dream, indifputably fignifies the Babylonian or Affyrian Empire.

" The breaft and *arms* of filver"— the *Medo-Perfian* Empire.—The arms are generally fuppofed to fignify the *two* kingdoms of the Medes and Perfians, which united, and deftroyed the Babylonian, and formed the Perfian Empire.

" The belly and thighs of brafs"—

---

[s] It appears from antient coins and medals, that cities and people were often reprefented by figures of men and women. A great terrible human figure was therefore an emblem of human power and dominion, and the various metals of which Nebuchadnezzar's image was compofed, may be fuppofed to typify the relative importance of the various kingdoms which fhould arife in the world. Newton, Diff. 13.

the Grecian Empire.—The Greeks were famous for their brazen armour.—The belly is supposed to distinguish the Macedonian Empire under Alexander; and the thighs, the Syrian kingdom under the Seleucidæ, and the Egyptian kingdom under the Lagidæ, or Ptolemies; which were *two* of the *four horns* which we shall find came up in the place of the *great horn* of the he-goat, that is, two of the divisions of Alexander's dominions after his death—the other two, Macedonia and Bithynia, were soon subdued by these, and became parts of their kingdoms.

" The legs of iron, and the feet of iron mixed with clay"—the Roman Empire in *all* its states.—The two legs of iron are supposed by some to mean the two Roman Consuls; and it is certain that the similitude of the Consular government was continued after the government became Imperial; for the Emperors

perors had almoft conftantly *Affociates* in the Empire, befides continuing the form of the Confular magiftracy.—It is in harmony with the Prophet's explanation to fuppofe the iron legs to denote alfo the ftrength with which this Empire fupported the vaft weight, which it obtained by conqueft over the three former kingdoms.

" The feet of iron mixed with clay," I fuppofe to mean the *eaftern* and *weftern* Roman Empires; for the Empire was certainly immediately *weakened* when it was thus *divided*—"it became partly *broken*, or *brittle*."

" The ten toes" were ten kingdoms which arofe afterwards, *all within* the bounds of the *antient Roman Empire*— " The iron was mixed with miry clay, to denote, as fome think, a peculiar degree of defilement during thefe periods of its exiftence, or " the mixture of barbarous

barous nations with which the Roman people was defiled." But the latter suppofition is not, I think, at all probable. The Jews interpret, "and they fhall mingle with the feed of men," as alluding to the mixture of Jews (emphatically termed *men*) with all thefe nations, which yet remain *diſtinct* from them—" do not cleave one to another, even as iron is not mixed with clay."

Suppofing the *feet* to be the *divided Empire*, the *ten toes* muſt belong to *both parts* of it; we are *not* therefore confined to the *weſtern* Empire for the *ten kingdoms*.

We muſt, I think, conclude, that the defcription of this image contains the hiſtory of the Roman Empire in all its ſtates; but nothing is faid to Nebuchadnezzar of an *eleventh* kingdom. Information concerning *this* kingdom, which was to be of a different kind, that is, partly of a fpiritual nature—and the power of which was to be exerted *within* the Empire, and *while* it fubfifted in its *laſt form* of ten kingdoms, was re- ferved to be given to the Prophet.— The *fate* however of this fourth Empire, is imparted to the monarch; as that of the three former Empires had been.— " A ftone cut out without hands, fmote the image upon his *feet*, that were of iron and clay, and brake them to pieces." -

"'Then was the iron, the clay, the brafs, the filver, and the gold, broken in pieces together, and became like the chaff of the fummer threfhing-floor, and the wind carried them away, that no place was found for them; and the ftone that fmote the image became a great mountain, and filled the whole earth." " In the days of thefe kings

' Dan. ii. 35, &c.

(that

(that is, of the *four* great kingdoms, for the three former had *not* been *destroyed*; their *sovereignty* was gone, but "their *lives* were prolonged for a season and a time[u]") shall the God of heaven set up a kingdom, which shall never be destroyed; and the kingdom shall not be left to other people, but it shall break in pieces and consume all those kingdoms, and it shall stand for ever. Forasmuch as thou sawest the stone that was cut out of the mountain without hands, and that it brake in pieces the iron, the brass, the clay, the silver, and the gold.

As the fourth or Roman Empire is described in its several states; so is the fifth kingdom, or the kingdom of the Messiah, described in its two states. Mr. Mede distinguishes these by the name of *regnum lapidis*, the kingdom of the

---

[u] See Sir I. Newton.

stone, and *regnum montis*, the kingdom of the mountain.

This kingdom was set up by the God of heaven, " when Christ came into the world"—*He* was " the stone cut out of the mountain" without human means, *while* the Roman Empire was strong as iron; but it did not smite the image till a *later* period, when it had *feet* of iron mixed with clay;" and then the *power* of the feet was soon *broken* into ten parts, or toes, in which 'state it' yet exists. The Empire was *divided* before the *visible* conquest of Christ over " the dragon," or the power of *Pagan Rome*, by the establishment of Christianity in the Empire.

" The powers of darkness were *then* shaken," but (as we shall find when we consider the little horn in the vision of Daniel) they are suffered to remain in a weakened state *till* " the *stone* shall become

come the *mountain*, and fill the whole earth," when " the kingdoms of the world shall become the kingdoms of the Lord, and of his Christ."

The kingdom of the mountain is then to be considered as yet *entirely* future.

Second Vision.——*The* FOUR BEASTS.

The four Empires which were exhibited to Nebuchadnezzar in the form of a great and terrible image, were represented to Daniel in the shape of great wild animals—such emblems and hieroglyphicks being usual among the eastern nations. This vision is much more particular in its descriptions—mentions many circumstances relating to each kingdom, and points out an extraordinary power, not even named in the dream of the image, which was to arife *during* the *laſt* ſtate of the fourth or laſt kingdom—was to continue " until a time, and times, and the dividing of time," (that is, 1260 years according to the common interpretation) but *not beyond* the duration of theſe kingdoms of " iron mixed with miry clay;" becauſe the *kingdom of the mountain* is to *deſtroy every* adverſe power, and is itſelf to reign over the *whole earth*: and we have ſeen that it was to ſtrike the whole image down to the ground, when in this *laſt* period of its power, and to eſtabliſh itſelf in its room.

The firſt beaſt, or the Babylonian or Aſſyrian Empire, is repreſented " like a lion with eagle's wings," " the wings whereof were plucked" at the time of the delivery of this Prophecy in the reign of Belſhazzar, for the Medes and Perſians were then encroaching upon it.

[59]

The second beast, or the Medo-Persian Empire, is "like to a bear, and it raised itself up on one side, and it had three ribs (or tusks) in the mouth of it, between the teeth of it; and they said unto it, Arise, devour much flesh."

It is well known that the Persians soon "raised themselves up" above the Medes, and that they were remarkable for cruelty and oppression. The three ribs (or tusks) in the teeth of this voracious animal, are supposed to be the kingdoms of Babylon, Lydia, and Egypt, which greatly strengthened the Empire[x], but which were dreadfully oppressed by it.

The third beast, or the Grecian Empire, is "like a leopard, which had upon the back of it four wings of a fowl; the beast had also four heads." The leopard

[x] See Bp. Chandler, and Sir I. Newton.

is a spotted animal, and remarkable for its swiftness, and is therefore a striking emblem of the different manners of the nations whom Alexander commanded, and of the rapidity of his conquests. Some think the four wings are designed for Assyria, Media, Persia, and Grecia— others, Persia, Greece, Egypt, and India, as well as to denote peculiar swiftness. The four heads are evidently the four kingdoms, into which the Empire was divided after the death of Alexander, because the four horns of the he-goat are thus explained by the angel. " And dominion was given to it," " sheweth," as Jerome saith, " that it was not owing to the fortitude of Alexander, but proceeded from the will of the Lord"......" and indeed unless he had been thus assisted, how could he in so short a time have brought all the countries, from Greece as far as India, into subjection [y]."

[y] Newton, vol. i. c. 14.

The fourth beaft, or the Roman Empire in all its ftates, "is dreadful and terrible, and ftrong exceedingly, and it had great iron teeth," " and nails of *brafs*," "it devoured and brake in pieces, and ftamped the refidue with the feet of it; and it was *divers* from all the beafts that were before it, and it had ten horns." This beaft was fo great and horrible, that no name was found for it— it had no fimilitude to any *known* beaft. The Roman Empire was of a different nature and conftitution of government from all the former kingdoms; and the length of its *duration*, and the *variety of forms* it was to affume, would fcarcely admit of its being called by *any* particular name fufficiently defcriptive.— " The ten horns" of this beaft correfpond with the " ten toes" of the image; and the " nails of *brafs*" denote the long continuance of fome fort of connexion between the *Roman* and the *Grecian* Empires; or rather, I apprehend, that

that the Roman Empire fhould in part exert itfelf under the name of a Grecian power: and this was in fact the cafe, when the Roman Empire was *divided*, if not when Conftantinople became the capital.

Thus far the Monarch's dream and the Prophet's vifion exactly agree. But another fubject is now introduced before the folemn mention of the time when " all thefe thrones were to be caft down," and " dominion and glory, and a kingdom that all people, nations, and languages fhould ferve him, were to be given to the Son of man, for an everlafting dominion;"—a conclufion as exactly fimilar to the conclufion of the dream.

While Daniel was contemplating " the ten horns, behold, there came up among them another little horn, before whom there were *three* of the firft horns plucked

plucked up by the roots: and behold, in this horn were eyes like the eyes of a man, and a mouth speaking great things." Daniel was greatly disturbed by this vision, and anxiously enquiring into its meaning, the angel answered, " These great beasts, which are four, are four kings (or kingdoms), which shall arise out of the earth" (or as it should be translated *in* or *upon* the earth—Daniel had seen these beasts symbolically arise from the sea; the angel speaks of them now in plain language as *empires*) " but the saints of the Most High shall take the kingdom, and possess the kingdom for ever, even for ever and ever."—Still was he anxious for a more *particular* explanation of the fourth beast, which was " so exceeding dreadful," " and of the ten horns that were in his head, and of the *other* which came up, and before whom three fell, even of that horn that had eyes, and a mouth that spake very great things, whose look was more stout

than

than his fellows."—" I beheld," fays the Prophet, whofe attention feems to have been fixed upon this object of the vifion, " and the fame horn made war with the faints, and prevailed againft them ; *until* the Antient of days came, and judgment was given to the faints of the moft High; and the time came that the faints poffeffed the kingdom."—And the angel thus anfwers his repeated enquiries; " The fourth beaft fhall be the fourth kingdom upon earth, which fhall be *divers* from *all* kingdoms, and fhall devour the whole earth, and fhall tread it down and break it to pieces.—And the ten horns out of this kingdom are ten kings, (or kingdoms) that fhall arife; and another fhall arife *after them*, and fhall be *divers* from the firft, and he fhall fubdue three kings. And he fhall fpeak great words againft the moft High, and fhall wear out the faints of the moft High, and think to change times and laws : and they fhall be given

into

into his hand, *until* a time, and times, and the dividing of time. But the judgment shall sit, and they shall take away his dominion, to consume and to destroy it unto the end. And the kingdom and dominion, and the greatness of the kingdom under the whole heaven, shall be given to the people of the saints of the most High, whose kingdom is an everlasting kingdom, and all dominions shall serve and obey him. *Hitherto is the end of the matter.*"—The angel's interpretation of this vision plainly extends to the end of the world[z]. This account of the little horn I consider then as an *epitome* of the *whole history of Antichrist.*—Keeping this idea in view, let us proceed to the next vision, which *selects* the second and third

[z] It may be observed, that the account of the little horn precisely resembles an episode in an epic poem—the history of the four kingdoms was given without it in the *image*; but *here* it is described as rising out of the *last*, and contributing to the catastrophe.

kingdoms, i. e. the Perſian and the Grecian, and a " little horn which came forth out of one of the four horns [a] of the He-goat, " or the King of Grecia," to form a *diſtinct* picture of a particular train of events, which we are thus naturally led to ſuppoſe will take place in the *eaſtern* part of the world.

Third Viſion——*The* RAM *and the* HE-GOAT, *including* "*the* LITTLE HORN" *of the Eaſt.*

In the former viſion, which was a general hiſtory of the four kingdoms, Per-

---

[a] The ſource of this figure, of *horns* for kingdoms, as Spanheim obſerves, muſt be derived from the Oriental languages, in which the ſame word ſignifies a *horn*, and a *crown*, and *power, ſtrength,* and *ſplendour*. A horn was an emblem of royalty among the Phœnicians, and the Chaldee Paraphraſts explain the Hebrew word *keren, a horn,* by the term *malcbutba,* which ſignifies a *kingdom.* Newton, c. xv.

ſia

fia was defcribed as a *bear*, to mark its *character* for cruelty and oppreffion. In *this*, which fhews only the rife, progrefs, and decline of *two* of the kingdoms, apparently with a view to the *principal* subject of it—*the little horn*, which was to arife after them—Perfia is defignated by its common fymbol, a ram [b].

" Behold there ftood before the river,

---

[b] It was ufual for the kings of Perfia to wear a ram's head made of gold, and adorned with precious ftones, inftead of a diadem; for fo Ammianus Marcellinus defcribes them. Bifhop Chandler and others farther obferve, that ram's heads with horns, one higher and the other lower, are ftill to be feen on the pillars at Perfepolis." Newton.

The goat is made the type of the Grecian or Macedonian Empire, becaufe the Macedonians were denominated *Ægeadæ*, or the goat's people, 200 years before the time of Daniel —It is alfo remarkable, that Alexander's fon by Roxana was named Alexander *Ægos*, or the fon of the goat: and fome of Alexander's fucceffors are reprefented in their coins with *goat's horns*. Newton.

a ram

a ram which had two horns, [Media and Perfia] and the two horns were high, but one was higher than the other, and the higher [Perfia] came up laſt. I ſaw the ram puſhing weſtward, and northward, and ſouthward, [it had poſſeſſion of the Eaſt] ſo that no beaſt might ſtand before him, neither was there any that could deliver out of his hand; but he did according to his will, and became great. [as in the time of Xerxes and Darius.] And as I was confidering, behold, an he-goat came from the weſt [the king, or rather kingdom of Grecia] on the face of the whole earth, and touched not the ground: [he came with ſuch *bounding rapidity*, that he ſeemed not to touch the ground] and the goat had a notable horn between his eyes. [Alexander king of Macedon, who had firſt ſubdued Greece.] And he came to the ram that had two horns......and ran unto him in the fury of his power. And I ſaw him come cloſe unto the ram, and

he

he was moved with choler againſt him, and ſmote the ram, and brake his two horns, and there was no power in the ram to ſtand before him, but he caſt him down to the ground, and ſtamped upon him: and there was none that could deliver the ram out of his hand. Therefore the he-goat waxed very great: and when he was ſtrong, the great horn was broken; [Alexander died at the height of conqueſt, and in the prime of life] and for it (or, inſtead of it) came up four notable ones toward the four winds of heaven. [Alexander's four Captains, who divided his kingdom; Caſſander held Macedon, and Greece, and the *weſtern* parts—Lyſimachus had Thrace and Bithynia, and the *northern* regions; —Ptolemy poſſeſſed Egypt and the *ſouthern* countries—Seleucus obtained Syria and the *eaſtern* provinces.] And out of one of them came forth a little horn, which waxed exceeding great, toward the ſouth, and toward the eaſt, and

and toward the pleasant land. And it waxed great, even to the host of heaven; and it cast down some of the host, and of the stars to the ground, and stamped upon them. Yea, he magnified himself even to the prince of the host, and by him the daily sacrifice was taken away, and the place of his sanctuary was cast down. And an host was given him against the daily sacrifice by reason of transgression, and it cast down the *truth* to the ground; and it practised, (or wrought) and prospered." To this description I subjoin the explanation given by the angel, previous to any observations upon it—" And in the latter time of their kingdoms, [that is, of the four kingdoms which succeeded Alexander's kingdom] when the transgressors are come to the full, a king of fierce countenance, and understanding dark sentences, shall stand up. And his power shall be mighty, but not by his own power: and he shall destroy wonderfully,

derfully, and shall prosper, and practise, and shall destroy the mighty and the holy people. And through his policy also he shall cause craft to prosper in his hand, and he shall magnify himself in his heart, and by peace shall destroy many: he shall also stand up against the Prince of princes, but he shall be broken without hand. And the vision of the evening and the morning [an Hebraism signifying a day] is true: wherefore shut thou up the vision, for it shall be for many days."

"[c] This little horn is, by the generality of interpreters both Jewish and Christian, antient and modern, supposed to mean Antiochus Epiphanes, king of Syria, who was a great enemy and cruel persecutor of the Jews; but then all allow that Antiochus Epiphanes was a type of Antichrist." Bishop Newton however, adopting the opinion

[c] Newton, c. 14.

nion of Sir Isaac Newton, leaves Antiochus wholly out of the question, and applies it to the Roman power, which first subdued Macedon and Greece, the capital kingdom of the goat, by which, he says, *the Romans became a horn of the goat*. But notwithstanding his very ingenious Dissertation[d] upon this subject, I cannot but think there remain as great reasons for applying this Prophecy in the first instance to Antiochus Epiphanes, and in the last to Antichrist, without contradicting the accuracy of its application, in *many points*, to the Romans. The plan of this Work obliges me to refer the Reader to Bishop Newton's Dissertation for a clear display of the fulfilment of this Prophecy, both by Antiochus and by the Romans; for it appears to me that he *establishes* the antient opinion even while combating it, from his earnest wish to *appropriate* the Prophecy *wholly* to the Romans: a wish,

---

[d] Newton, vol. ii. Diss. 15.

which

which too often rifes unperceived even in the beft minds, who, when they form a fyftem, defire to fubvert every other. —I muft content myfelf with a few obfervations, connected with the endeavour to *harmonize* thefe fyftems, and to point out the *connexion* of the Prophecies.

In the main points of oppofition to Chrift and of perfecution of his fervants, all the branches of Antichrift muft *necef- farily agree*; but the marks which diftinguifh *thefe confederate powers* from each other, appear to me very ftrongly difcriminated in thefe different vifions.—*All* foretel the power of Antichrift, and contain allufions perhaps to *all* the different forms of that power; but *each* vifion feems to defcribe *one* of thefe forms with *peculiar diftinctnefs*, while it points to *fome* circumftances which ftrongly characterize *that* Power which was to arife the *laft*, and, if we rightly conjecture, will prevail the moft, and which are not

eafily

easily appropriated to either of the other. The symbol of " a little horn" is applicable to Antichrist in the *beginnings* of all its forms—Papal, Mahometan, and Infidel.—The Power of Antichrist is still the little horn; but as exerted in Greece and the *East*, it is described as the little horn of the *he-goat*, or the *third* empire, and this even to the present hour; for the *seat* of the *Mahometan* Empire is *Grecia*, or what was called the *Greek Empire*.—As exerted in Italy and the *West*, it is described as the little horn of the *fourth* beast, or the *fourth Empire*. But it is remarkable that in those predictions, which the angel *expressly* declares will be accomplished *towards the* end *of the appointed time*, this distinction of east and west seems to be *lost*, both in this and in the following vision (which I conceive intended to *particularly* describe the Mahometan and Papal powers), and Antichrist appears with all the subtilty and fury and universally-extended tyranny,

ranny, with which we find him delineated in the Revelations under the fymbol of the *fecond* beaft, and which correfponds with the little horn in the vifion of the four beafts, which will be noticed hereafter—And this circumftance, I apprehend, intimates the *general* apoftafy and perfecution which is to take place during the infidel power, which was to *fucceed* the violence of the two former, and be an *inftrument of punifhment* to their adherents, and of *trial* to the Church of Chrift.

It is evident from the conclufion that this Prophecy cannot be *confined* to the Romans. It extends not only beyond the deftruction of Jerufalem, but to the end of time; for, as "the image was to be broken by the ftone cut out without hands," and the fourth beaft was to be deftroyed " becaufe of the great words the horn fpake againft the moft High;" fo *this* horn was to be broken without hand,

hand, becaufe "he rofe up againſt the Prince of princes." And it is farther added, as if to prevent the Prophecy from being *reſtricted* to its *firſt* and *partial* accompliſhment, "Shut thou up the viſion, for it ſhall be for *many* days"—it refers to a long period of time, and feries of events, and it cannot therefore be fully underſtood till much nearer the time of the end.—Let us now compare the Mahometan power with this little eaſtern horn, which "waxed exceeding great toward the fouth, and toward the eaſt, and toward the pleaſant land."

The Mahometan power has indeed extended itſelf *fouthward* over great part of Africa—*eaſtward* to Perſia, Tartary, and even China, and covered *the land of Judea* with its abominations; but it never made any progreſs in the weſt or north—"It caſt down fome of the hoſt, and of the ſtars, and ſtamped upon them, and magnified itſelf even to the prince

prince of the hoft," or "the Prince of princes." It caft down many of the *reigning powers*, took poffeffion of the Greek empire, and overthrew all the Chriftian churches, or *ftars*[e], eftablifhed in Africa, in Arabia, and India, and almoft all in Paleftine, in Afia Minor, and in Greece.—Mahomet acknowledged Jefus to be a Prophet indeed; but he affumed to himfelf a fuperiority in dignity; and the cruelty, oppreffion, and contempt, with which Chriftians have been uniformly treated by his followers, are plainly denoted by his " ftamping upon them." Jerufalem is defignated as the principal fcene, or object of the tyranny of this horn; firft during the Jewifh, and laftly during the Chriftian difpenfation. Zion was the place chofen by the Almighty for the *only* Temple devoted to his worfhip according to the Mofaic ritual—in this favoured fpot was the Gof-

[e] Rev. ii.

pel

pel firſt publiſhed to the whole world. *Here* was the one oblation once offered of the Lamb ſlain for the redemption of mankind—and *here* was the Chriſtian church firſt eſtabliſhed—Antiochus took away the " daily ſacrifice" for a few years.—The Romans put an end to the Temple worſhip—but the Mahometans have profaned the place of his ſanctuary—" have taken away the daily ſacrifice of praiſe and thankſgiving" from this diſtinguiſhed land, for above eleven hundred years.—It was alſo " *given* into their hands by reaſon of tranſgreſſion;" this was acknowledged by the Jews and by the Romans[f] in the two former caſes; and the deplorable corruption of the eaſtern churches, when this horn aſſumed the form of Mahometaniſm, ſufficiently explains *why* an " hoſt was given againſt them".—This horn has indeed " caſt the truth to the ground"—for

[f] See vol. i. p. 296.

nothing

nothing can be more miserable than the internal as well as external state of the few churches which remain in the countries under the Mahometan yoke, and the Jews suffer little less oppression than the Christians.—And the artifices by which this hypocritical impostor and his successors established the civil and religious power of Mahometanism, and their astonishing success, can scarcely be more strongly marked than by the expression, "it *practised* and *prospered*," but which expression is not easily made applicable to the Romans.

Thus ends Daniel's account of the vision; but he adds, that he heard one saint, or angel, ask another angel, " How long shall be the vision concerning the daily sacrifice and the transgression of desolation, to give both the sanctuary and the host to be trodden under foot ?" Or, as Mr. Lowth renders it more clearly, " For how long a time shall the vision last, the daily sacrifice be taken away, and the transgreffion of desolation continue to give both the sanctuary and the host to be trodden under foot?" And it was answered, "Unto 2300 days: then shall the sanctuary be cleansed." Both the question and the answer are distinctly put, and resemble Rev. xi. 2. but there is an uncertainty in the number of years; the Seventy read 2400; and Jerom informs us others read 2200. If the vision be computed from the establishment of the Persian Empire, which begins the vision of the ram, the reading of the Seventy will carry it on to the conclusion of the sixth millennium of the world. However this may be, it is remarkable that this vision breaks off abruptly; the *end* of *this* horn is not *seen*, it is left in prosperity, a circumstance which accurately corresponds with the description of the *same power* in the ninth chapter of the Revelations. We do not see the *end* of *Abaddon*, or *Apollyon*, the King of the Saracen Locusts,

Locusts, or of the Turkish horsemen from the river Euphrates—but it is to be remembered we are elsewhere told, that "the *sixth vial* shall be poured out upon the river Euphrates, to *prepare* the way for the kings"—about which time it is also said; "the sanctuary shall be wholly cleansed," and "the bride made ready to receive her lord."

When the angel Gabriel was sent to *explain* this vision to Daniel, he begins with saying, ". Understand, O Son of Man: for *at the time of the end* shall be the vision," which I presume to mean, the train of events described in this vision shall reach to the end of time. And after he had prepared the Prophet to receive the awful information, he further says, " Behold, I will make thee know what shall be *in the last end* of the indignation; for at the time appointed the end shall be"—meaning I again presume, I will not only explain the general

neral meaning of this vision, which is itself a series of punishment, but I will inform thee of other circumstances, which shall take place when the time *of this vision of indignation*, or wrath against the host and the sanctuary, *shall draw near its conclusion*—for the time is *appointed*, and the *end* of all this misery shall certainly come; and therefore take comfort from this assurance, while I reveal the awful judgments which are to take place *in the last days* of the vision."—" The ram which thou sawest having two horns, are the kings of Media and Persia. And the rough goat is the king of Grecia, and the great horn that is between his eyes is the first king. Now that being broken, whereas four stood up for it, four kingdoms shall stand up out of the nation, but not in his power."—The angel barely mentions the kingdoms of Persia and Grecia and the four kingdoms which were to arise after Alexander, and then *immediately* passes to *the latter*

latter time of their kingdom—as if they were only mentioned to mark *the scene of action* for the formidable power which is the principal object of the message—he omits those circumstances described by the vision, which point to its *primary* and partial accomplishment by Antiochus and the Romans, and which the Prophet probably understood to relate to calamities similar to that which his people were then suffering under the power of Babylon; and goes *directly* to that *distant* period which had been before represented as so *peculiarly* dreadful in the vision of the little horn, which arose from the fourth beast.

We are then, I conceive, authorized to conjecture, that the following description points out not *only* the Mahometan power, but refers to that *other* power which was to immediately precede the time of the end; or, in other words, be the *last form* of *Antichristian power*.

power.—" *And in the latter time* of their kingdom, when the transgressors are come to the full, a king of fierce countenance, and understanding dark sentences, shall stand up;" it is certain that the power of Mahomet arose in a part of the *Grecian Empire*—and that he arose when the *eastern division* of the *Roman* Empire was considered as the *Greek Empire*, and in the *latter time of that kingdom.* It is certain too, that the corruptions of the eastern churches had arisen to their full height, when this scourge of the Christian world stood up; —and that "the false Prophet, or Teacher," of Arabia, who professedly propagated his religion by the sword, is strikingly delineated by " a king of fierce countenance, and understanding dark sentences."—" And his power shall be mighty, but not by his own power." As the kingdoms of the West gave their power to the Beast, or Papal Antichrist, so have the kingdoms of the East given theirs

theirs to the Mahometan Antichrist. But I conceive this is not all that is here meant—" The dragon" gave his power to the beast, and " the angel of the bottomless pit" led on the Saracenic locusts; and thus the angel may be understood to say, " The power of this horn shall be not merely that which is common to the conquerors of the East, such as the he-goat, or the four beasts in the former vision; it is to be directed and supported by super-human art and strength; which shall enable it to destroy *wonderfully*, to prosper and practise, and destroy the mighty, and the holy people," that is, both Jews and Christians. —" And through his policy also he shall cause craft to prosper in his hand," or " shall cause fraud and deceit to prosper, and he shall magnify himself; and by peace shall he destroy many," or, " in times of tranquillity he shall destroy multitudes[f]." The *policy* and *craft* for which the Mahometan powers are noto-

[f] Wintle's Version of Daniel.

rious[g], unqueftionably agree with this defcription; and the titles which their chief affumes, of "*God on Earth, the Shadow of God,*" *Brother to the Sun and Moon,* "*The Giver of all Earthly Crowns*[h]," as perfectly accord with the Prophetic intimation, that he fhould "magnify himfelf." Such titles were indeed common in the Eaft, among the antient *Heathen* potentates; but they are utterly inconfiftent with true religion, and have ever been fo confidered by Jews and genuine Chriftians—the titles however affumed by the *Pope*, are ftrikingly fimilar.—The multitudes which, allured by promifed "peace," left the crofs of Chrift for the crefcent of Mahomet; and the luxury, effeminacy, and licentioufnefs, which are the allowed habits and propofed rewards of the followers of this pretended Prophet, may perhaps be

[g] "In a word, luft, arrogance, covetoufnefs, and *the moft exquifite hypocrify*, complete their character." Maundrell, p. 149.

[h] See Ricaut's State of the Ottoman Empire.

allowed to explain " by peace he shall destroy many :" but as this power is yet existing, we may surely suppose it may hereafter become more clear, *if* this be not perfectly satisfactory. The angel having thus intimated, as I apprehend, that this formidable power should remain some time *at rest* as it were, adds, " And he shall *also* stand up against the Prince of princes, but he shall be broken without hand"—The persecuting spirit of Mahometanism certainly corresponds with the opposition implied in this expression, marks its *origin*, and *distinguishes* the motives and views which actuate this power, from those which are the common causes of war and conquest among the rulers of the earth, but can hardly be considered as its full import. —If this expression be confined to the Mahometan power, we may look to the future for a more literal accomplishment, and suppose the angel to say, " *Besides* these wars against the *sanctuary* and the holy

holy *people*, and the *covert* mifchief which he fhall be permitted to do, this power fhall *at laſt openly direct* his oppofition againſt the Prince of princes—then will the time come when he fhall fall before him, like the image and the other horn in the former vifions." This paſſage however, and feveral others in the latter part of this Prophecy, will be found to agree very remarkably with the *diſtinct picture* which I underſtand to be given in the Revelations, of the *Infidel power*; and if thefe paſſages be allowed to refer to *that* as well as to the Mahometan power, the meaning of the angel may be then fuppofed to be, " The power, of whom I *now* fpeak, who is to arife in *the latter times,* fhall fpring from the *fame fource,* and be of the *fame nature* as the little horn in the former vifion— and *his mark* fhall be, *oppofition* to *the Prince of princes,* as it was in the horn of the fourth beaſt.—By this fhall thefe *peculiar* powers be diſtinguiſhed from the

the kings of the earth, and by *this* shall their common fate be foreknown—they shall be broken without hand—not by the usual course of events—but they shall fall before the Son of man, when he cometh to take possession of his kingdom"—" And the vision of the evening and morning is true. Wherefore shut thou up the vision, for *it shall be for many days.*"—Surely this repetition confirms the opinion that these predictions concern the *latter times.*

Fourth Vision.—" The KING" *of the West.*

In the following vision the angel first declares,. " Now I am come to make thee understand what shall befal *thy people* in the *latter days*; for *yet the vision is for many days.*"—Daniel had been previously informed of the precise time

when

when the Meffiah was to appear, and when "he fhould be cut off, though not for himfelf;" and alfo, of the fubfequent deftruction of the city and the fanctuary, and " of the defolations determined *unto the end of the war*, even unto the confummation, and that determined fhall be poured out upon the defolate," or as it is in the margin of the Englifh Bible, " upon the *defolator*[h]."

I fhall

[h] My plan confines me to that part of this wonderful Prophecy, which appears to relate to Antichrift—or "*the war* between the Dragon and the Lamb," (fee Rev. xii.) but I muft beg the Reader to perufe the fixteenth of Bifhop Newton's Differtations, to fee " how particular and circumftantial it is concerning the kingdoms of Egypt and Syria, from the death of Alexander to the time of Antiochus Epiphanes. There is not fo complete and regular a feries of their kings, there is not fo concife and comprehenfive an account of their affairs, to be found in any author of thofe times. The Prophecy is really more perfect than any hiftory. No one hiftorian hath related fo many circumftances, and in fuch exact order of time, as the

Prophet

I shall begin the observations I presume to offer with the passage which is considered as relating both to Antiochus and to the Romans, who had just subdued Grecia, when they commanded Antiochus to return home—" For the ships of Chittim¹ shall come against him,

Prophet hath foretold them : so that it was necessary to have recourse to several authors, Greek and Roman, Jewish, and Christian, and to collect here something from one, and to collect there something from another, for the better explaining and illustrating the great variety of particulars contained in his Prophecy........The exactness of this Prophecy was so convincing, that Porphyry could not pretend to deny it, and therefore asserted, that it could not possibly have been written before, but it must have been written in, or soon after the time of Antiochus Epiphanes.......Others after him have asserted the same thing, not only without proof, but contrary to all the proofs which can be had in cases of this nature. Newton, Diss. 16.

¹ The coast of *Chittim* and the land of Chittim is a general name for Greece, Italy, and the countries and islands of the Mediterranean—The countries

him, therefore he shall be grieved and return, and have indignation against the holy covenant: so shall he do: he shall even return, and have intelligence with them that forsake the holy covenant. And arms shall stand on his part," or as it may be more clearly rendered, "And after him arms (that is, the Romans) shall stand up"—Wintle renders it, "But mighty powers shall stand up *from these*," that is, from the *descendants of Chittim*—"and they shall pollute the sanctuary of strength, and shall take away the daily sacrifice, and they shall place the abomination that maketh desolate;" to which passage our Saviour refers in his prediction of the destruction of Jerusalem[k], and therefore *fixes* its *ultimate reference to that event.*—History fully authorizes us to apply a part of what fol-

tries peopled by *Cittim*, the son of Javan, the son of Japhet.—See Newton's fifth Dissertation; Bochart, Vitringa, and Wintle.

[k] See vol. i. c. 10.

lows

lows to the times of Antiochus Epiphanes in its primary fenfe, and with him I prefume the *double* links of this connecting chain conclude; and the hiftory of the church is then continued from the deftruction of Jerufalem to the general refurrection.—" And fuch as do wickedly againft the covenant fhall he corrupt through flatteries; but the people that do know their God, fhall be ftrong, and do exploits. And they that underftand among the people (by which is to be underftood the Chriftians) fhall inftruct many: yet they fhall fall by the fword, and by flame, by captivity, and by fpoil, many days. Now when they fhall fall, they fhall be holpen with a little help: but many fhall cleave to them with flatteries. And fome of them of underftanding fhall fall, to try them, and to purge, and to make them white—even to the time of the end: becaufe it is yet for a time appointed." We have here predictions of the perfecutions to which

the

the Christians were subjected, with little interruption, for the first 300 years, and of the help afforded them when fallen to the lowest state of depression, by the establishment of Christianity in the Roman Empire. This is called *little help*, because the church was raised only to that degree of prosperity suited to a state of trial, and continued but a short time to enjoy it; for it was soon corrupted by those who " clave to it by flatteries," or worldly motives.

There was however a remnant left amidst this general apostasy; and many churches were again established " by them of understanding," to whom *the little help* was also given at the time of the Reformation; but being still " the appointed time" of indignation—of the reign of Antichrist, and of warfare to the church—they were left to struggle with their various enemies; and it is expressly declared, " that *some* of them

them should fall—not so much for *punishment* as for *purification*—for *a time only*, and *not for ever*. And we may farther observe, that this Prophecy seems to intimate that *some* of these churches should *stedfastly resist* these attacks, and *be enabled* " to stand before the Son of man," at his coming to destroy the works of Satan, and to establish his church in everlasting perfection, glory, and security.— Thus have we a summary view of the history of the Christian church " till the time of the end" of that tribulation which is so frequently the subject of Prophecy. But the angel reverts to what appears to be the principal object of his mission—to forewarn the church of the *nature* and *conquests* of its enemies—to guard it against the *varied* efforts of its antagonist—to afford a solid ground for *faith* and *hope* to rest upon, when assailed by the most furious storms of the conflicting elements, deceit and rage, superstition and indifference, ignorance

norance and *philosophism*, which satanic art should be allowed to raise *within the period* allotted for the reign of Antichrist.

It was observed, that as "the little horn" in the former vision was said to spring from Grecia, we should naturally look to the *eastern* part of the world for the scene of its action. Similar reasons will now lead us to suppose that *the king* now mentioned in this vision, was to arise and display his power in the *west*. For the angel has brought down the history to the taking of Jerusalem by the *Romans*; and we know the *Roman Empire* was at that time the *reigning power*. " The *king*" therefore thus mentioned, without any epithet or distinguishing appellation, we must conclude to be a *Roman Power.*—" And the king shall do according to his will; and he shall exalt himself, and magnify himself above every god, and shall speak marvellous

vellous things againſt the God of gods, and ſhall proſper till the indignation be accompliſhed: for that that is determined ſhall be done. Neither ſhall he regard the God of his fathers, nor the deſire of women, nor regard any god: for he ſhall magnify himſelf above all. But in his eſtate ſhall he honour the God of forces; and a God whom his fathers knew not ſhall he honour with gold, and ſilver, and with precious ſtones, and pleaſant things. Thus ſhall he do in the moſt ſtrong holds with a ſtrange God, whom he ſhall acknowledge and increaſe with glory: and he ſhall cauſe them to rule over many, and ſhall divide the land for gain. And at the time of the end ſhall the king of the ſouth puſh at him: and the king of the north ſhall come againſt him like a whirlwind, with chariots, and with horſemen, and with many ſhips; and he ſhall enter into the countries, and ſhall overflow and paſs over. He ſhall enter alſo into the glorious land, and many countries ſhall be be overthrown: but thefe fhall efcape out of his hand, even Edom, and Moab, and the chief of the children of Ammon. He fhall ftretch forth his hand alfo upon the countries: and the land of Egypt fhall not efcape. But he fhall have power over the treafures of gold and of filver, and over all the precious things of Egypt: and the Libyans and the Ethiopians fhall be at his fteps. But tidings out of the eaft and out of the north fhall trouble him: therefore he fhall go forth with great fury to deftroy, and utterly to make away many. And he fhall plant his tabernacles of his palaces between the feas, in the glorious holy mountain; yet he fhall come to his end, and none fhall help him."

"And at that time fhall Michael ftand up, the great prince which ftandeth for the children of thy people: and there fhall be a time of trouble, fuch as never was fince there was a nation even to that fame time: and at that time thy people shall

shall be delivered, every one that shall be found written in the book. And many of them that sleep in the dust of the earth shall awake, some to everlasting life, and some to shame and everlasting contempt. And they that be wise shall shine as the brightness of the firmament; and they that turn many to righteousness, as the stars for ever and ever." The application of this Prophecy to the *Papal* Antichrist—to the conquests of the Saracen king of the south, and the Turkish king of the north, over the holy land and many other countries—the escape of Arabia, and the subjection of Egypt and Barbary have been clearly, I had almost said *indisputably*, established by many learned Commentators. But how far this Prophecy may be considered as a *double type* of Antichrist, and how much may be supposed to be *yet future*, are questions that can only be decided by a careful comparison with *other* Prophecies respecting *the same period*, and by the course of events which *time* shall bring to light. Mr. Wintle's tranflation gives a more clear view of what I confider as the *primary* object of this Prophecy, than the common one; I shall therefore beg leave to ftate it, with a few obfervations connected with the leading ideas of this chapter.

" For *ftill*, for *an appointed time*, a (or *the*) king shall even act according to his will, and shall exalt himfelf and magnify himfelf above every god, and againft the God of gods shall he fpeak marvelloufly, and shall profper until the completion of the indignation: for the decifion is made."

This " king" is conftantly allowed to mean Antichrift, who shall poffefs himfelf of the *Roman* power of which the angel has been fpeaking, and affume defpotic authority both in *civil and religious* matters, and shall occafionally exalt himfelf *above all laws human and divine*. Yet it shall profper *till the indignation*

dignation shall be completed; that is, probably till the days of vengeance against the Jews shall be accomplished [k]," " and the fulness of the Gentiles shall be come in;" for *till then* " the witnesses are to prophesy in sackcloth;" or the church is to remain in a state of suffering and trial.—" Also to the gods of his fathers shall he not attend." This power, though not a faithful worshipper of the true God, shall pay no attention to the polytheism of his Roman ancestors—he shall not attend either, to the established Christian religion, but shall corrupt it with his own vitiated mixtures;—" nor to the desire of women, nor to any god shall he attend, but shall magnify himself above all." " The desire of women" is interpreted by Mr. Mede and Bishop Newton, as relating to the conjugal state, or the desire or affection for wives; and seems to be placed in this description of Antichrist, not merely as a striking feature of Monkish and Papal insti-

[k] Wintle and Mede.

tutions,

tutions, but to *diftinguifh* this power from the Mahometan horn defcribed in the former vifion.—A *difregard* to the holy inftitution of marriage is indeed ftrikingly applicable to both Popery and Infidelity—but not to Mahometanifm, where it is held in high eftimation, according to antient cuftoms and eaftern manners—" Yet near to God in his feat fhall he honour Mahuzzim [or God's protectors] even *near the God whom his* FATHERS [the antient Romans] knew not, fhall he do honour, with gold and with filver, and with precious ftones, and with the moft defirable things. And he fhall provide *for fortreffes of Mahuzzim, together with God, whom he fhall certainly honour*, and caufe *them* to have dominion over many; for the land will he diftribute at a price." For the application of this moft accurate defcription of the Papal power of Antichrift, I refer the Reader to the following Chapter upon that fubject.—" But *at the time of the end*, a king of the fouth fhall pufh

at

at him; alfo a king of the north fhall tempeftuoufly rufh upon him with chariots and with horfemen, and with a large fleet, and fhall enter into the countries, and fhall overflow and pafs through. *He* fhall enter alfo into the land of glory, and though many fhall be ruined, there fhall efcape out of his hand Edom, and Moab, and the chief of the Ammonites. Yet when he fhall extend his power over the countries, the land of Egypt fhall not efcape; but he fhall have dominion over the treafures of gold and of filver, and over all the defirable things of Egypt; and the Libyans and Ethiopians fhall be in his fteps. But rumours fhall difturb him from the eaft, and from the north; therefore he fhall go forth in great fury to deftroy and devote to utter perdition many. And he fhall fix the tents of his pavilion between the feas in the mountain of the glory of holinefs; yet, he fhall come to his end, and no one fhall help him. Moreover at that time fhall shall rise up Michael, the great prince that standeth up for the children of thy people; then shall there be a time of trouble, such as never was since the existence of a nation until this time; and in this time shall *the people* escape[1], every one that is found written in the book. Then multitudes that sleep in the dust of the ground shall awake, some to life everlasting, and others to reproaches, to confusion everlasting. And those that have wisely instructed shall shine like the splendor of the firmament, and those that have made many righteous, like the stars for ever and ever. But thou, Daniel, close the words, and seal up the book, until the time of the

[1] By this passage I apprehend is meant, not only the return of the Jews from their dispersion, but the "escape" of the holy people of God, not only Jews, but Gentile Christians; according to many passages in Scripture relative to that time, which indicate that at this time of *peculiar judgment*, the good shall be *distinguished* from the wicked. See our Lord's predictions and revelations, &c.

end :

end: when many shall have searched diligently, and knowledge shall be increased." The accomplishment which the former part of this Prophecy has received in the conquests of the Mahometan power, is confessedly accurate—but much remains to be fulfilled; and many reasons might be produced to authorize the conjecture, that even *that part* of the Prophecy will hereafter receive a more *full* and perfect accomplishment.—The change is so abrupt, that it is *yet* difficult to decide, whether by "HE shall enter also into the land of glory," be meant " the king of the north" [the Turks in particular], or " the king" first mentioned, that is, *the power of Antichrist*, which is *the principal subject of the Prophecy in another form*[m].—Of one thing

[m] Dr. Doddrige remarks, in his note on our Lord's Prophecy, "Jerusalem shall be trodden down, till the time of the Gentiles be fulfilled," that "the time of the Gentiles," means " the time when they shall be *visited*, and *punished*," and this accords with the time of the reign of Antichrist. He farther observes,

thing however we are certain, that the "end" of *this king*, whether Mahometan, or Infidel, is to be exactly similar to the end of the *Grecian* little horn, and the horn of the *fourth* beast in the former visions; "yet he shall come to his end, and none shall help him." We may likewise presume, that the end of this king shall take place at the *same time* with that of these little horns, and with the recal of the Jews from their dispersion, which is mentioned according to the angel's promise to inform Daniel "'what should befal his people *in the latter days*."

The conjecture therefore that these are all branches of the SAME power, that

observes, "Thus the Turks, *or some other* Antichristian Power, may continue possessed of the Holy Land till the restoration of the Jews: for we can hardly suppose their way to it should then be opened by the conquest of a *Christian* power." Of one thing however we are certain, that the " end" of *this* " *King*," whether Mahometan or Infidel, is to be exactly similar to the end of the Grecian little horn, &c.

must

muſt together *die*, when their root is deſtroyed, is thus far confirmed.

The INFIDEL POWER *a third Branch or Form of Antichriſt ſhewn to be predicted by Daniel.*

I ſhall now take leave to ſuppoſe that I have ſhewn the Mahometan as well as the Papal Antichriſt to be clearly depicted in the Prophecies of Daniel.—It remains to be examined whether the Infidel Antichriſt was not as accurately drawn in the picture, though unobſerved till the ſtrong reflected light thrown upon it by recent events brought out the lines. The objects firſt in chronological order were firſt preſented to our view. And that this ſketch of the Infidel power, which we ſhall find was afterwards more minutely finiſhed, was not *intended* to be diſcovered till *near the time of the end*—the time for its appearance is, I think, evident from the injunction of the angelic meſſenger. "But thou, O Daniel, ſhut up the words, and ſeal the book, *even to the time of the end*"—then "many ſhall run to and fro; and *knowledge ſhall increaſe*."—And when Daniel "heard" the declaration of the angel concerning "the *time* of the end of theſe wonders, but underſtood not," and aſked for an explanation, he was anſwered, "Go thy way, Daniel: for the words are cloſed up and *ſealed till the time of the end.* Many ſhall [*then*] be purified and made white and tried: but the wicked ſhall do wickedly: and none of the wicked ſhall underſtand, but the wiſe ſhall underſtand"—or as Wintle renders this paſſage, "But though none of the wicked *will attend*, thoſe of underſtanding *ſhall attend*." How far the preſent circumſtances of the world indicate the arrival of this promiſed period of increaſing knowledge of the Prophetic writings, it well becomes each in his generation to conſider.

The

The Reader will recollect, that when considering the vision of the beasts, and the little horn which arose *among* or *after* the ten horns, it was observed that this vision probably contained a description of *the whole of Antichrist*. The distinct pictures which we have since seen of the Mahometan and Papal Forms of this power, appear to confirm this idea. And when we reflect upon the superior solemnity of the conclusion of this first vision, it will, I think, seem probable, that in this general description, the *last* of the forms it was to assume would be the *most* particularly noticed, if any were particularized above the rest. We shall find, I think, upon examination, that this was really the case[m]. It has already been

---

[m] Whether the ten horns of the beast are *literally* ten kingdoms, or whether the number ten signifies only that the Roman Empire was to be broken into *many* parts, and that during the existence of these *numerous* kingdoms the little horn should arise, is a question

been stated, that these ten kingdoms do *not* appear to *necessarily* belong to the *western* division of the empire; and it seems clear that *this broken form* is to remain till " the judgment is set." We are therefore at liberty to suppose, that *this* little horn, which is Antichrist, represents both the Mahometan power in the *East*, and the Papal power in the *West*; which were in fact raised up nearly together: and if the description of this horn be found fairly applicable to *another* power which was to arise *afterwards, within the bounds of the antient Roman Empire* (as we gather from the consideration of *other Prophecies*), we may as naturally conclude that it was designed to represent *that power also*. If this be

---

question not easy to decide.—The supposition of the indefinite number would remove a difficulty generally felt by all Expositors; but, as Archbishop Secker observes, " it doth not appear that any of the numbers in Daniel mean uncertainty;" and therefore it must be admitted with caution.

granted,

granted, and surely it can hardly be denied, the different opinions of Commentators respecting this little horn, so far from being discordant, will be found in unison; and more loudly sound the harmony of Prophetic truth.

Those who see the Mahometan power in "the little horn," which arose from the fourth beast, generally suppose Egypt, Asia, and Greece, to be "the three horns plucked up by the roots before it." Bishop Newton[n], in his application of this Prophecy to the Papal power, considers them to be the exarchate of Ravenna, the kingdom of Lombardy, and the state of Rome; and observes[o], that the Pope hath in a manner pointed himself out for the person described, by wearing the triple crown."—We can at present form no opinion concerning the *three* horns which are to be *eradicated* by the

[n] Note, Diss. 14.
[o] Newton, vol. i. p. 485.

Infidel

Infidel power; whether abfolutely *kingdoms* be meant, or whether *independent ſtates* may be confidered as a fufficient explanation—but pofterity may be enabled to decide upon this fubject perhaps more clearly than the partial fulfilment of this Prophecy has hitherto enabled us to do, refpecting the conquefts of the Mahometan and Papal powers.

In order to fhew that the application of this Prophecy to the Infidel power of Antichrift, fo far from doing any violence to *received interpretation*, does in fact more *fully* exemplify, more *accurately* accord with it; in all fuch circumftances as the fhort time that has elapfed fince its developement will allow us to difcern, I fhall fhortly ftate Bifhop Newton's explanation, as he refers the defcription to the Papal power [p].—" And behold, in this horn were eyes like the eyes of a man,

---

[p] Newton, vol. i. p. 487.

and

and a mouth ſpeaking great things"—"The eyes of a man denote *his cunning and foreſight*, his looking out and watching all opportunities to promote his own intereſt"—the perſpicacity and cunning of this power, who is *penetrating in myſterious craft*[q]. "He had a mouth ſpeaking very great things"—"thundering out his *bulls* and *anathemas*—excommunicating princes, and abſolving ſubjects from their obedience."—"His look was more ſtout than his fellows"—"*his aſſumed ſuperiority* over his fellow Biſhops, and Kings, and Emperors"—"And he ſhall ſpeak great words *againſt* the moſt High" (or, as Symmachus renders it, "*as* the moſt High," which is as appropriate to the Papacy, as *againſt* is to Infidelity)—"*ſetting up himſelf above all laws divine and human*; arrogating to himſelf godlike attributes, and titles of holineſs and infallibility, *exacting obedience to his ordinances and decrees*, in preference to, and in *open violation of reaſon, and Scripture*,

[q] Wintle, &c.

in-

infulting men, and blafpheming God."—" And he fhall wear out the faints of the moft High"—" *by wars and maffacres, and inquifitions; perfecuting and deftroying the faithful fervants of Jefus, and the true worfhippers of God*, who proteft againft his innovations, and refufe to comply with the idolatry practifed in the Church of Rome"—*And he fhall think to change times and laws*—" appointing fafts and feafts, canonizing faints, granting pardons for fins, inftituting new modes of worfhip, impofing new articles of faith, enjoining new rules of practice, and *reverfing at pleafure the laws both of God and man."*

And now let the unbiaffed Reader judge, whether this defcription of the little horn of the fourth beaft be not *more ftrikingly applicable* to the *Infidel* power, which we have feen arife in France, than even to the Papacy of Rome?—If St.

^p This fubject will be more fully examined in the fourth Chapter of this Volume.

Paul's

Paul's description of "the Man of Sin" be found equally applicable (and that it is, has been satisfactorily shewn by Mr. Jones [q])—if the second beast in the Revelation, which has hitherto baffled enquiry, appears from examination to be the *exact*, and as it were the *appropriate* type of this same recently-risen power—a power which the antient Prophets and the Apostles of our Lord repeatedly declare was to arise " in the LATTER TIME *of the time appointed for indignation* [r]"—*in the latter times*, in the *last days*—we cannot surely require more evidence of the justness of the application—We shall be no longer " shaken in mind" at the progress of such amazing wickedness, when

[q] In two Sermons printed in 1794, and 1795, at the desire of numbers who were struck with the truth of the application.

[r] Even if we date the *beginning* of these days of vengeance from the destruction of Jerusalem, the Papal and Mahometan powers, which arose together about the year 600, or 750, cannot be considered as *completely* fulfilling this Prophetic intimation.

we

we fee that it is fulfilling the "fure word of Prophecy," and "underſtand what is to be the end thereof."

The general Opinion concerning the SECOND BEAST *in the Revelations, conſidered to be erroneous.*

It muſt be confeſſed, that the numerous interpretations concerning the ſecond beaſt mentioned in the Revelations of St. John, are neither compatible with each other, or ſatisfactory in their application.—And this acknowledgment very confiderably ſtrengthens the opinion, that this hieroglyphic creature delineates a *Power* as diſtinct from Popery, as Popery is from Mahometaniſm, but which *Power* had not a *viſible* exiſtence when moſt of theſe interpretations were written. According to the mode of explanation moſt commonly adopted,

adopted, there appears *a degree of repetition* in the Prophecy, and a defcription of the *fame thing* in different words, and in different ways, which we do not feem authorized to conclude is really the truth. —For it fhould be obferved, that to defcribe the *fame appearance* of a power in various ways, is totally different from defcribing the *fame power* as *appearing* under *different forms*, at *different periods of time.* " The Pope and his Clergy," for example, is furely *only* the *Papal Power fixed at Rome*[s]. " The Greek Church," which was once Sir Ifaac Newton's idea, cannot be a right application, becaufe it feparated from Rome *before* that city became the feat of the Papal Empire. The *firft* beaft is confidered by Daubuz, as denoting the Antichriftian *civil* powers which were to be within the Roman Empire, during the fecond period of the church; and the fecond beaft as denoting the Antichriftian *ecclefiaftical*

[s] See Mede, Whifton, Newton, Waple, &c.

powers

powers during the same space of time; and therefore he supposes the "two horns" to be the lines of the Bishops of Rome and of Constantinople.—Lowman considers the second beast to be "the Holy Roman Empire" established in Germany. Vitringa regards it as the Inquisition, and the Dominican and Franciscan orders of Monks.—Bishop Newton, Whiston, Pyle, Bishop Hurd, and Dr. S. Clarke, consider the first as the "secular beast," or the *Civil power* of the Papal Empire of Rome, acting not only at Rome, but by its ten horns, or ten kingdoms, which were formed after the first Empire was broken by the northern nations; and they suppose the *second* beast to be the *Ecclesiastical* power of Rome.

There are indeed many objections to these interpretations, besides *sameness* in the beasts, and *repetition* of representation.—The *first* beast of the Revelations, and the little horn of Daniel,

niel, are generally allowed to mean the *fame power*, whatever that power may be.—Now if *only* the *civil* power be defignated, in what was the Antichriftian horn *divers* from the other ten horns? Four horns, or heads, arofe out of the *Grecian* kingdom, two of which foon fubjected the two others.—There is nothing therefore remarkable in the *coming up* of the little horn; it is either the *kind* of horn that is extraordinary, or the *circumftances under which it arifes.* We are told [t], " All the world wondered after the" (*firft*, or what is termed by Newton and other Commentators, the *fecular*) " beaft."—The world was too much accuftomed to Afiatic and Roman defpots, to *wonder* at *civil tyranny*. It furely muft have been its monftrous coalition with epifcopacy—its being " feated in the temple of God, fhewing himfelf as God, and fpeaking great things and blafphemies"—*profeffing the religion*

[t] Rev. xiii.

of

of the Lamb, and yet *perfecuting* his faithful fervants, which excited fo much aftonifhment.—" The mouth that was given unto this beaft, fpeaking blafphemies, and the power to make war with all the faints and to overcome them," defignates the perfecuting fpirit and power of *Ecclefiaftical Rome* in this firft general defcription; but when the beaft appears again[u], with the woman (or "the great city," as this fymbol is explained by the angel) fitting upon it, *thefe* marks of the beaft are omitted, and the *woman* is defcribed as " arrayed in purple, and drunken with the blood of the faints and martyrs."—And it cannot, I think, be eafily fuppofed, that the woman and the fecond beaft reprefent *the fame power*, which by implication they muft do according to thefe interpretations of its meaning.—We fee then the *union* of the civil and the ecclefiaftical power of the Church of Rome, both in the little

[u] Rev. xvii.

horn

horn of Daniel [x], and in the first beast of the Revelations.—We may observe too, that the *Dragon*, the emblem of *Pagan* Rome, " gave his power to *this* beast," which I conceive to represent the junction of *idolatry* with *civil* and *religious tyranny*, and this must indeed seem *wonderful* in a professedly Christian Church.

Another reason for believing the second beast in the Revelations a Power *distinct* from the first, is, that there are many passages in the Apostle's description of " the perilous times in *the last days*," which can hardly be applied to the *Papal* or the *Mahometan* Antichrist, and certainly not to *Civil tyranny* unconnected with religion.

It is remarkable, that in the first Epistle to Timothy, St. Paul's predic-

---

[x] And particularly in the *Roman* "king."

tion relative to " the *latter times*," applies in every particular to the *Papal* Antichrist—And that in the *second* Epistle he says, " This know *also*, that *in the last days* perilous times shall come, for men shall be [y], &c." In the application of these words to *a later period of time*, we are authorized by the opinion of a most profound and sagacious interpreter of Scripture. It is observed by Joseph Mede[z], " that the last times, simply and in general, are the times of Christianity; the last times in *special* and *comparatively*, or the latter times of the last times, are the times of the apostasy under Antichrist."—And we have, I think, clearly seen that " the *latter end* of the days of vengeance," which are " the times of the apostasy under Antichrist," are occasionally *expressly distinguished*. The se-

[y] See 2 Tim. iii. and the four first verses of the fourth chapter, quoted page 5.
[z] Mede's Works, p. 804.

cond and third chapters of the second of Peter, and the Epistle of St. Jude[a], do certainly belong as little to the Papal power of Antichrist.—But do we know of no Power in *these present days*, to which this description will most accurately apply? Is it possible to draw a more exact picture of APOSTATE INFIDELITY, united with DEMOCRATIC TYRANNY? And if upon examination, we find any corresponding marks of this dreadful power in the second beast of the Revelations, having already seen them in the Prophecy of Daniel, will not this agreement add so much weight to the separate testimony of each, as altogether to be nearly demonstrative evidence to the truth of the opinion and the justness of the application?

But though, from the various circumstances already stated, we cannot be sur-

---

[a] See page 16—23.

prized

prized that moſt of the learned Commentators have failed in their attempts to explain a Prophecy reſpecting events which to them were veiled by futurity, we have the authority of *ſome*, who, either unfettered by ſimilar prejudices, or endowed with ſuperior ſagacity, formed conjectures concerning the ſecond beaſt, which at once excite our admiration, and confirm the opinion which is now offered to the conſideration of the publick.—The Biſhop of Meaux and the learned Grotius approached more nearly to the truth than has been uſually imagined, when they ſuppoſed the ſecond beaſt to denote PHILOSOPHY, " falſely ſo called."—Dr. Hartley, in the concluſion of his Obſervations on Man, conſiders " INFIDELITY as the Beaſt."—It ṣ alſo his opinion, that when the world ſhall be arrived at a certain degree of *depravity*, it will then be prepared for " the *times of deſolation*."—Sir Iſaac Newton, and Dr. Clarke, interpreted " the

reign

reign of the Beast" to be " THE OPEN AVOWAL OF INFIDELITY".—They farther conjectured, that " the state of religion in *France*, and the manners of the age, combined with the Divine Oracles to announce the *approaching reign of the Beast*"—And they considered it as probable, that the Ecclesiastical Constitution of *France* would soon be subverted, and that the standard of Infidelity would be first set up *there*[b]." And they

---

[b] See the conclusion of Hartley's Observations on Man, published by G. Nicol—Whiston's Life, and Clarke's Works.—The conjecture formed by Mr. Fleming concerning the destruction of the *French Monarchy* under the fourth vial, before, or about the year 1794, printed nearly a hundred years ago, remarkably coincides with this conclusion—with recent facts—and with the general idea of the Prophetic writings contained in this chapter. Lowman, Bishop Newton, and several others have looked to *France* as the scene of some great change, or some dreadful event that would particularly affect the church of God.

supposed Rev. xi. 7. to relate to this important æra in the Christian world.

" And when they[c] [the two witnesses] shall have finished their testimony, [or shall be *finishing*, or be *about to finish*, their testimony—and they were to prophesy the same number of years as the first beast, that is, 1260] the beast that ascendeth [that is, *ascendeth*, or *is ascending* AT THE TIME that the witnesses are *finishing* their testimony] out of the bot-

[c] Whether Fleming's opinion respecting " the witnesses" be equally well founded with his conjecture relative to France, must remain a question. He supposes " the witnesses were slain" immediately before the Reformation, and " ascended up to the heaven of rest and security when the Protestant Churches were established." This opinion, with which Bishop Newton and many other learned Commentators concur, is very consolatory at this period of general attack; but I confess it appears to me to be attended with too many difficulties to be adopted with confidence.

tomless

tomlefs pit, shall make war against them, and shall overcome and kill them."—It will appear evident that the beast thus described is the same with the second beast of the thirteenth chapter of Revelations which " afcendeth out of the *earth,*" when we consider the numerous passages in Scripture which indicate that " the bottomless pit" does *not* mean *the same as the sea.* And this point will be found to throw confiderable light upon the subject as we proceed in our endeavours to investigate it.

The INFIDEL POWER *of Antichrist shewn to be predicted also in the Revelations.*

It is considered as an established point, that the beast with seven heads and ten horns, and the woman upon whose forehead

head was written, " Myftery, Babylon the great, the mother of harlots, and abominations of the earth," denote the Papal Antichrift, whofe feat is Rome, and that the duration of this Antichriftian Power was to be 1260 years.—The difficulty has been to underftand the meaning of " the beaft which comes up out of the *earth*—had two horns like a lamb, and fpake as a dragon, exercifeth all the power of the firft beaft before him, and caufeth the earth and them that dwell therein to worfhip the firft beaft whofe deadly wound was healed," —deceiveth many by means of miracles [*wonders*] which he had power to do in the fight of the beaft, faying to them that dwell in the earth, that they fhould make an image to the beaft which had the wound by a fword and did live— and had power to give life unto the image of the beaft; that the image of the beaft fhould both fpeak, and caufe

that

that as many as would not worship the image of the beast, should be killed; and he caused all, both small and great, rich and poor, free and bond, to receive a mark in their right hand, or in their foreheads, and that no man might buy or sell, save he that had the mark, or name of the beast, or the number of his name. Here is wisdom. Let him that hath understanding count the number of the beast. For it is the number of a man; and his number is six hundred threescore and six[e]."

The first beast arose out of the *sea*,

---

[e] Various have been the conjectures concerning this mystical number—*Vicarius Filii Dei*, a title which the Popes have assumed to themselves, and caused to be inscribed over the door of the Vatican exactly makes 666, when decyphered according to the numeral signification of its constituent letters. *Lateinos* (the word mentioned by Irenæus), *Romiith*, and *Ludovicus*, each contains the same number. See Pyle on the Revelations, p. 103. and Fleming, p. 140.

that is, in prophetical language, *out of*, or *during*, violent commotions, wars and tumults, or times of violence and troubles.—The second beast arises out of the *earth*, that is, according to general interpretation, exactly the reverse of the first description—*rising gradually* in times of calm and quiet, like a plant out of the earth, which establishes itself imperceptibly by a thousand roots, before it shews its head, and *silently* attains its destined height and strength—This beast has " two horns like a lamb." Horns are the acknowledged symbols of strength or power—the first beast has ten horns, which are explained by the angel to be ten kingdoms which gave their power to the beast, and thus increased his *civil* power.

But the horns of the second beast are of a *peculiar kind*, they are " like a lamb, or the lamb," which symbol throughout the Revelations represents Christ—It is this

this which has especially led to the opinion that the second beast is the *Ecclesiastical* power of Rome, because these horns must denote *something* which *seems* to be like Christianity—they are not said *to be* the horns of a lamb, but *like,* or *resembling,* the horns of a lamb.

"He speaks (however) *as*" in the same manner with "*a dragon,* or *the dragon.*" As words proceed from the heart, or soul, or mind, which are truly the man, the *real nature* of this personage is thus declared in very plain terms, and so are the *arts* by which he shall obtain and support his power.

It appears then, that this second beast is *not* to wear the form of civil tyranny, but is to derive his power or strength from its *semblance* to the religion of Christ, or the Lamb; by which it will deceive many (who are elsewhere said to be under the influence of " strong delufion, and to believe a lie"), and will *thus* gain poffeffion of public opinion, though this " feducing form of godli- nefs" breathes in reality " the doctrine of devils."—It is ufually underftood that this fecond beaft is called[f] " the falfe *Prophet,*" or *Teacher,* which was taken with the (firft) beaft,—and[g] " the beaft that arifeth out of the bottomlefs pit" (or " hell, in which the dragon is afterwards bound") " and that maketh war againft the witneffes, overcometh and killeth them."—This defcription agrees perfectly with that of his rifing out of the *earth,* but (unlefs the pit and the fea mean the fame, which I think they cannot mean) *not* with that of the beaft which rifeth out of the fea.—It agrees alfo with the power of the fecond beaft to *give* power to the *image* of the firft beaft, to *caufe* that as many as would not worfhip the image of the beaft fhould

[f] Rev. xix. 20.   [g] Rev. xi. 7.

be

be killed."—This second beast did *not appear* to make the image of the first beast himself, but he *caused them that dwell in the earth* to make it: having first *deceived* them into obedience to his will by means of the miracles or *wonders*, which he had power to do in the sight of the first beast; that is, before the expiration of the 1260 years, or within his kingdom.—And so absolute and universal was his sway, that " small and great, rich and poor, bond and free," " *were deprived of all commerce with men, and civil privileges of life, if they did not in some way or other make profession of obedience to his constitutions and decrees*[h]," and adopt some sign, or wear some mark denoting their enrolment into the service of the beast and his image, by which they are themselves formed into an *affociation or fraternity*.—And all men are considered and " *treated as worthy of*

[h] Lowman, p. 190, but applied by him to the Pope.

death,

death, who refuse an entire submission, in any particular, to these decrees[i]." The second beast, and the image *to which he gives life*, are then PERSECUTING powers. This second beast " exerciseth *all* the power of the first beast," that is, his tyranny extends over the *minds* as well as the *bodies* of men—their *spiritual* as well as their *temporal* interests—their *religious* as well as their *civil* liberties—he was "to make war with the saints and to overcome them, and to have power over all kindreds, and tongues, and nations."

Daubuz observes, that "the powers constituting the first beast, or Papal Rome, carried on the *same design* against true religion, though in another form, as the *dragon* did when the empire was Pagan." "It was the *dragon* who gave power to the first beast who spake great things and blasphemies; and all that dwell on the earth worshipped the dragon.

---
[i] Lowman, p. 190.

gon and the beast, except those whose names are written in the book of life of the Lamb slain from the foundation of the world." And the second beast has also the power of the *dragon*, whose *spirit dictates his words*, or doctrines and commands—but this connexion, the *real origin* of his power, is now more concealed from the world, who are not so much *subdued*, as *deceived* into subjection; for it is to be remarked, that this second beast has no marks whatever of civil power—The counterfeit likeness to the Lamb seduces them at first to believe that his power is from heaven, " because of the wonders that he doth in their sight," to expect from him universal happiness, and by degrees to follow his orders *implicitly*, however contradictory to his pretensions to *true morality, truth*, and *genuine religion* (which indeed must ever *include* moral virtue) till they are led " to make an image by his direction," which shall punish their credulity

dulity and wickedness by the most cruel and exceffive tyranny, while it is held up to them as the idol of their *affections*, or their *worſhip*; and to which, by a ſtrange infatuation, they *continue* to yield a willing obedience, notwithſtanding the miſeries it creates. " They blaſphemed the name of God, which hath power over theſe plagues; and repented not, to give him glory[i]."

This image is made to *reſemble* the *firſt* beaſt, but it is wholly unconnected with it, except as they both belong to Antichriſt—It is the *ſecond* which *gives it life*, and *directs its operations*—It is called the *image* of the firſt beaſt—which ſignifies the ſame union of tyranny, blaſphemy, and idolatry, *openly exerted*; which it is to be obſerved, the ſecond beaſt does not *avow*, or *appear* to exert or maintain, but *ſecretly produces and upholds* in the image which he cauſed to be made.

[i] Rev. xvi. 9.

made. The form of the firſt beaſt, it ſhould be remarked, was made up of the four beaſts that repreſented to Daniel the four great empires of the earth; but there is ſome change in the order in which they are mentioned—It is not *impoſſible* but this order may be in future found applicable to the *courſe of its conqueſts* over the kingdoms they originally repreſented; for the ſecond beaſt is to have power over all kindreds, and tongues, and nations, " by *means of the image* made like the firſt.—We may then ſuppoſe that the *Image* has ſeven heads with the name of blaſphemy, and ten horns with crowns upon them"—the ſeven heads are explained by the angel to repreſent the *Roman* Empire, and *forms of government*[k]—the ten horns with crowns, the ten kingdoms into which the empire was broken[l], and the crowns ten kings over them which were " to receive pow-

[k] See note, p. 147.
[l] See Daniel's Prophecy, p. 64, 58.

er one hour with the beast," "to give their power to him for a time, but afterwards to turn against the seat of his tyranny[k]." It is like "unto a leopard," signifying *swiftness*, and a motley mixture of people—and in Daniel's vision the *Grecian* Empire.—" Its feet are as the feet of a bear," cruelly stamping on all its prey, and standing in the former vision for *Persia*—" its mouth as the mouth of a lion"—which represented *Assyria*, or *Babylon*—itself the well known type of *Antichristian Rome*, because of its pride, blasphemy, and cruel treatment of the servants of God; and which crimes are particularly marked by the *mouth* of the lion, whose tremendous roar " maketh all the beasts of the forest to quake."

[k] Nothing is here said of the fall of three of these horns—as the *little horn* appears now in its *full power*, as *the beast*, that period of its history must be supposed to be passed; and I confess there being *still ten*, inclines me to suppose that ten denotes an indefinite number.

" It

"It has a mouth speaking great things and blasphemies, and it opens its mouth in blasphemy against God, to blaspheme his name, and his tabernacle and them that dwell in heaven."—The deadly wound of one of the heads of the first beast—the ten kings giving it their power for a time, and then making war against it—the conquest of the three kingdoms mentioned by Daniel, and the power given him by the dragon against the saints, are not properly *descriptive of himself*, but *circumstances* of his *history*, which may or may not belong to the history of the image, but with which however the history of the image will in some respects probably be found to agree.

Here then in this IMAGE, set up by *the power of the* DRAGON, we find displayed to our view, the same tremendous *union* of *civil* and *religious tyranny* which the first beast possessed, supported by the *falsehood* and *imposture* of the second beast

beast who caused it to be made by the dupes to his artifices.—The same blasphemy against God and his church, and his faithful servants—the same *despotic* rule over the earth in civil and religious affairs, *must be visible* in this image. But it does *not* necessarily follow that this persecuting power should adopt the same *mode* of persecution—proceed upon the same *principles*, or direct itself against the same persons—It does *not* necessarily follow that it should speak *the same words* of blasphemy, or that its *despotism* should wear the *same form* as that which the first beast assumed.—And indeed, I cannot but think, that when the first beast and the image are compared with attention, it will appear that a *difference* in these respects is strongly marked; and that the reign of the *Image* of the beast is yet more tremendous in its effects upon the eternal interests of mankind, and even more generally oppressive in the exertions of its civil power.—It is

said

said of the first beast *generally*, that "all the world worshipped the dragon which gave power to the beast, and they worshipped the beast" *also*;—signifying the idolatrous spiritual power, and the temporal or secular power *united* in the seat of Rome.—But it is said of the image *particularly*, that " as many as would not worship this image, should be killed by it," and that it should cause all persons of *every rank and condition*, which are expressly *enumerated*, either to receive a mark, acknowledging their submission or attachment, or to be deprived of their civil rights and privileges.—Now it is declared by an angel in the following chapter, that "if any man worship the beast and his image, and receive his mark in his forehead, or in his hand, the same shall drink of the wine of the wrath of God, which is poured out without mixture *into the cup of his indignation:* and he shall be tormented with fire and brimstone in the presence of the holy angels, and in the presence of the Lamb:

and

and the smoke of their torment ascendeth up for ever and ever; and they have no rest day nor night, who worship the beast and his image, and whosoever receiveth the mark of his name. Here is the patience of the saints. Here are they that keep the commandments of God, and the faith of Jesus[1]."

It is worthy notice that the angel who thus denounced the wrath of God against the worshippers of the beast and his image, *followed* two others; the *first* of whom " flew in the midst of heaven, having the everlasting-Gospel to preach unto them that dwell on the earth, and calling upon them to fear God and give him glory, because the hour of his judgment was come."—And the *second* of whom declared " the fall of Babylon." Now the first of these angels is generally understood to represent the preaching of the Gospel, which was brought forth from its concealment at the time of *the*

[1] Rev. xiv. 9, 10, 11, 12.

Reformation; and which certainly did produce the *fall*, or *decline* of the power of Babylon; which is proclaimed by the second angel.—And as it is according to the merciful dispensations of God's Providence to give his servants *warning* of a near and imminent danger, it may be supposed that the *third* angel precedes the time of the *greatest* danger, and most severe trial; and thus the period of the *most tremendous* tyranny of *the* IMAGE, is fixed to be after the *Reformation*.—It should also be remarked, that *between* the descriptions of the two beasts we find the following call to particular attention to the *justice* of, the judgments of God in making his enemies instruments in his hand to punish each other; while the true church, his faithful servants, sometimes afflicted, and sometimes protected, wait " with patience and faith," to see the accomplishment of the mysteries of his word—for it is in this sense I understand these words.

" If

"If any man have an ear to hear, let him hear. He that leadeth into captivity fhall go into captivity, he that killeth with the fword, fhall be killed by the fword. Here is the patience and faith of the faints [m]."

This interpretation does certainly contradict the common opinion, that the fecond beaft is to fupport and advance the authority of the Church of Rome; but it muft be acknowledged to harmonize with the true fpirit of Chriftianity, and with the information which Scripture and Hiftory afford us concerning the moral government of the world; and, I think, it will be found to explain many of the difficulties attending the common application of this Prophecy.— But, it will be afked, how can this interpretation be made confiftent with the twelfth verfe of this chapter? "And he

---

[m] Compare Rev. xiii. 9, 10. with Dan. xii. 10.

exerciseth all the power of the first beast before him, and causeth all the earth, and them that dwell therein, to worship the first beast whose deadly wound was healed."—In answer to this objection, I beg to observe, that the *two verses* which immediately follow this summons to attention, contain *the whole description* of the beast and his power in *general terms*—the succeeding verses being an account of *the manner* in which he exerciseth his power, and are in some sort, both an *amplification*, and a *detailed repetition* of the former description.—These two verses therefore (the eleventh and twelfth) extend from the beginning to the end of the reign of the second beast; and, considering a great part of this reign *as yet future*, I must also consider it as impossible to ascertain the precise meaning of a Prophecy relating to that future.—All that can be done, and indeed all that ought to be attempted, is, to offer an explanation of this passage, and a conjecture refpecting it, which will be found to accord with this interpretation and with my general view of the Prophecy itfelf. The *form* and *nature* of this beaft have been already confidered; but the Reader will pardon fomething like repetition in Mr. Lowman's words[u], for the fake of his authority.

" I farther beheld in my vifions another appearance as of a fecond wild beaft *rifing* out of the earth, which had two horns like the horns of a lamb, but his voice was like that of a dragon, to reprefent *another perfecuting* government exercifing its authority with a fhew of meeknefs and charity, but carrying on the oppofition of the Devil, the old Serpent, to pure religion, and promoting idolatry by perfecution." Mr. Lowman proceeds to paraphrafe the twelfth verfe

[u] Lowman, p. 182.

thus:

thus; "And this second persecuting power had all the powers of the first, or *new revived form of Roman government*, and used its authority to spread the power of the *new Roman* government, beyond the bounds of its proper dominion, so as to oblige *the several nations* to yield obedience to the new authority revived in the city of Rome, after it had been so long deprived of all authority, and seemed to have lost all hope of recovering it."

It has also been already shewn in what manner we are to understand the second beast is said " to exercise all the powers of the first beast, before him[n]." And the angel's explanation of the seven heads[p]
will

---

[n] See page 127, &c.

[p] " And there are seven kings, five are fallen, and one is, and the other is not yet come; and when he cometh, he must continue a short space. And the beast that was, and is not, even he is the

will perhaps authorize us to suppose that the *worship*, which the second beast caused

eighth, and is of the seven, and goeth into perdition." These seven kings denote the seven forms of the Roman government—first Kings, second Consuls, third Dictators, fourth Decemvirs, fifth Military Tribunes, sixth Emperors, seventh Gothic Kings, and Exarchs of Ravenna, eighth Popes.— The sixth head, which was existing at the time of the vision, received " the deadly wound" from the hand of Odoacer in 476, when the Western Empire was completely destroyed and the government of Rome entirely changed.—" After a reign of sixty years the throne of the Gothic Kings was filled by the Exarchs of Ravenna, the representatives in peace and war of the Emperor of the Romans. Their jurisdiction was soon reduced to the limits of a narrow province, but Narses himself (the general of the *Eastern* Emperor Justinian), the first and most powerful of the Exarchs, administered above fifteen years the entire kingdom of Italy...... Under the Exarchs of Ravenna, Rome was degraded to the second rank." Gibbon, vol. iv. p. *313*. The *eighth* head was to be *of the seventh*, which was to endure comparatively but a short time, and had but little power. And we accordingly find the conqueror of Italy, Pepin, King of France, *invested*

the

caufed to be paid to the beaft whofe *deadly wound was healed*, alludes particularly to the *image* which he caufed to be made *in his form of civil tyranny.*— The feven heads reprefented feven mountains (the type of Rome), and *alfo* feven kings, or *forms of the Roman government;* —the head which received the *deadly wound* was the *imperial* or *monarchical* form of government; and great aftonifhment is expreffed that this mortal wound to the *civil power* fhould be healed in fuch a manner, that *Rome* fhould *regain* the poffeffion of this *civil power*, raife it to a *higher pitch of tyranny* than ever—exercife it in a *new manner*, and reign as *the Antichriftian beaft* over the whole world.—How far this expla-

the Pope, or fovereign Pontiff of Rome, with the *exarchate of Ravenna* in 756—and that foon after he became poffeffed of the *fovereignty of Rome*, and the *kingdom of Lombardy.*—Then was completed that union of civil and ecclefiaftical tyranny which conftitutes the reign of the Antichriftian beaft."

nation correfponds with the *hiftory* of the *image—the likenefs of the beaft*—let the Reader judge.—I fhall however, in fupport of the preceding interpretation[p], beg to obferve, that of the feven laft plagues which are poured out[q], there is *one*, and *but* one (which is poured out upon *the fun*, the emblem of *France* according to the general interpretation) which "*gives power* to the fun to fcorch men with fire."—The vials being *filled with wrath, muft torment the objects upon which they are poured out*; but it is evident that the fourth vial makes the *object* of its fury *alfo* the *inftrument* or *agent* of punifhment to others—that it is the *only* one that acts in this manner—and that this vial immediately follows a voice from the altar, praifing God for the " truth and righteoufnefs of his judgments," in having *judged* or *determined* that blood fhould be given to thofe to

[p] Rev. xiii. 9, 10.   [q] Rev. xvi.

drink,

drink, who had shed the blood of Saints and Prophets[r]. The power of the sun is, therefore, I imagine, to be the *means of darkening the kingdom of the beast*," which is the object upon which the *fifth* vial is poured out, and it *may also* be instrumental in some way or other, in executing the wrath which the sixth is to pour upon the river Euphrates[s]"—Its first office is "to *scorch* men with fire," and it is next to strike the inhabitants of the kingdom of the beast, " with *blindness*, and with *pains*, and *sores*," from its extreme heat; alluding to the well known effects of the sun in the hottest

---

[r] It is to be remembered, that I consider the seven vials as continuing in force, though not perhaps with equal violence, from their successive beginnings till the time of the end. And, I apprehend, that the voice from the altar refers as much to the succeeding, as to the preceding judgments of God. Many arguments might be adduced in favour of both these suppositions.

[s] This was written in the year 1797.

climates.—It is expressly said, that " the men who were scorched with great heat by the fourth vial, blasphemed the *name of God*, which hath power over these plagues, and repented not of their deeds, to give him glory," that is, did not acknowledge the justice of his judgments—perhaps even denied that they were *judgments*, attributing their sufferings to mere *secondary* causes.—It is also said that when the fifth vial was poured out, " they blasphemed *the God of heaven*," (indicating, I presume, a still bolder kind, or higher degree of blasphemy[t]) " and repented not of their deeds."—It cannot therefore be doubted that this

[t] It was asked by Bishop Prideaux, about the year 1650, " Whether Socinianism and slighting of all antiquity be not an introduction to Paganism and Atheism ?" Introd. to Hist. p. 155. fifth Edit. 1672. Barruel and Robison will convince us of the rapid progress made by Deism within the last fifty years towards *Atheism*, and " every evil work."

period,

period, during the violence of the fourth and fifth vials, *will be remarkable for* GENERAL *profaneness, and irreligion, and depravity of heart, and corruption of manners*, as well as for the *avenging* judgments of the Almighty; and, I confess, it appears to me little less certain, that the fourth, fifth, and sixth vials are contemporary with the *reign* of *the second beast and his image*—Let us now examine farther, how far the *character* of that reign will agree with the *character* of these vials.

I consider the second beast and his image to be connected just as the dragon and the first beast were connected.— The idolatrous spiritual power of the dragon was *visibly* exerted in ecclesiastical tyranny, which the world *saw* united with civil tyranny in the first beast.— But a great change having taken place in the earth before the *rising* of the second beast—" the *great city* having been

H 5 divided

divided into three parts," at the Reformation (that is, the three Confeſſions as they are called, Roman Catholic, Lutheran, and Calviniſt; ſee Jurieu and other Commentators) by which the power of the firſt beaſt was confiderably weakened, and the minds of men emancipated from the chains of ignorance and ſuperſtition which had held them enſlaved to the power of *Babylon*, " which *now* came up in remembrance before God"—the dragon raiſes up *another* beaſt, in a form better ſuited to the ſtate of the world towards the end of the time appointed for his reign.—For this beaſt is not to continue *beyond*, only *until* the termination of the 1260 years appointed for the dominion of Antichriſt—a great part of which term was expired before his reign commenced.

I am aware it has been objected, that as this diviſion of the great city is mentioned

tioned *after* the pouring out of the seventh vial, it cannot, without violating the order of time, be referred to the Reformation. But I conceive this earthquake to be a *particular judgment* upon the great city, or the power of Rome, rather than the *effect* of the seventh vial. If we compare Rev. xi. 13. we shall find the earthquake that destroyed the tenth part of the city, and 7000 men, took place *during* the *second* woe. For by *the same hour*, is to be understood *the time of the second woe*, or, according to the eastern mode of expression, " the reign of the angel of the second woe trumpet," alluding to an opinion, common in the East, that different angels, good or bad, were permitted to exercise authority during different portions of the day, and over different regions of the earth"[u]. Now

[u] Our Lord, accommodating his language to this popular opinion, says, " This is *your hour*, and the powers of darkness."

the second woe began when the Turkish Empire was established in 1005, or in 1299, and is yet in power; and there is nothing in this expression to *fix* this earthquake at *any particular time* within the hour[x]. From the context however, or rather from the course of events, I suppose this earthquake is to be placed *near* the *end* of the second woe, and *after* the earthquake which *divided* the city into three parts.—The earthquake mentioned Rev. xi. 19. I apprehend to be *distinct* from these, and to synchronize with the *third* woe, and the *seventh* vial, which is to have *universal* power and effect (being poured into the *air*, to de-

---

[x] In like manner "the three unclean spirits (Rev. xvi. 13.) out of the mouths of the dragon, the beast, and the false Prophet," must not be supposed to make their first appearance under the sixth vial. They might have been at work for a course of ages, but they would now unite their arts and powers, and be peculiarly active just before " the great day of battle." (Rev. xix. 19.)

note

note both its extensive operation, and the utter destruction of the Antichristian power—the air being represented in Scripture, as the seat of the power and authority of Satan), and to bring *sudden* destruction on all the enemies of Christ, when the seventh trumpet sounds the termination of the days of vengeance. Instead of breaking the order of time, this idea places the earthquakes in regular succession, marking the most striking events in the history of the church; and it will probably be confirmed, when we observe further, that when the earthquake, which divides the city into three parts, is mentioned, *nothing* is said of *the great change* made from misery to happiness, by the *finishing* of the days of wrath, or the sound of the seventh trumpet—on the contrary, it is expressly declared, " *Babylon* came up in remembrance before God," as if after having been suffered to pursue her career for some time unmolested, she was now to become the

parti-

particular object of punishment, and to receive the *first* "cup of the wine of the fiercenefs of the wrath of God." This firft earthquake I therefore fuppofe to reprefent *the time of the Reformation*, and am inclined to place it as contemporary with the *firft* effect of the fourth vial, poured out upon the *fun*, or ruling power, which was clearly the Pope, till "his city was divided," and then the king of France, who had given him his power and fplendour, arofe as he declined; but the ftorm which followed it, I confider as continuing to beat upon "the *men* who have the mark of the beaft [or Babylon], and who worfhip his image," to the prefent hour.—Many of "the *iflands*," or petty ftates in his peculiar territory are already loft, and *the mountains* of his ftrength are gone—The "great hail," the ufual fymbol of *the irruption of a barbarous people*, is now the plague of thofe men, who, having the mark of the beaft, by an extraordinary infatuation

worfhip

worship the image, which is the appointed agent of its destruction (*for this "hail falls from heaven"*), and yet "blaspheme the name of God, who hath power over these plagues." The Papal sun, though suffering a very considerable diminution of its own glory, "had power given it to scorch men with fire." Of this the history of the Reformation will furnish abundant evidence. The crown of France, which had been a zealous agent in the business of massacre and intolerance—witness St. Bartholomew's day, and many other scenes of blood—became the *acknowledged* Sun[z] of the political sphere in the reign of Louis the fourteenth, when it reached the meridian of its glory. This sun did also "scorch men with fire," as the revocation of the edict of Nantz, and the thousand barbarities which mark this vaunted *Augustan* reign, will amply testify. But the

[z] See Fleming, p. 53.

dregs

dregs of the cup of retaliation were now to be poured out upon this devoted kingdom—its Regal fun was blotted from the political heavens, and *a more tremendous Meteor* took poffeffion of the darkened fky.—Then did the *fecond* earthquake, " in which the tenth part of the city," or one of the ten kingdoms "fell," convulfe the earth. For I prefume the *fecond* earthquake to reprefent the Revolution in France, and at *that* period (that is, ftill under the fourth vial) I date the commencement of the reign of the *image*, though I conceive the fifth vial is now poured out, and conjecture that the fixth is near[a]. The confequences of *this* earthquake will be more generally felt, and excite more general terror than the plagues of the firft, fo that *at laft* the *remnant* will be affrighted, and *give glory to the God of heaven*, and thus they *perhaps* will find protection

[a] See note, p. 151.

from

from the effects of the *third* woe, and the feventh vial, which I imagine will fall with *peculiar* violence "upon them which deftroy the earth," by the united powers of Infidelity and Democratic tyranny, or, in other words, the fecond beaft, and the image.

Conclusion.

And now may I not afk, whether we have not ourfelves feen a Power gradually rife from its den, where it has long been ftrengthening itfelf, and from whence it has long fent forth the fumes of an intoxicating poifon to prepare the world for its appearance, which exactly refembles this fecond beaft? Have we not feen APOSTATE INFIDELITY under the name of REASON eftablifh its dominion over the minds of men by its pretenfions sions to a *refined* religion, a *pure* morality? Are not the doctrines of LIBERTY and EQUALITY, doctrines most perversely drawn from the *religion of the Lamb*[x], the HORNS of its *fascinating* power? Does it not unite the subtlety of the serpent, with the fury of the dragon?—promise universal happiness, but lead to universal misery? Has it not " caused them that dwell on the earth to make an IMAGE to (or *like*) the beast which had the wound by a sword and did live?" An IMAGE in the form of the *antient Roman* government, which has already obliged *many* of the nations to yield obedience to its new revived authority? —exerciseth all the *civil* and *religious* tyranny of the first beast, or the Papal power of Antichrist, by depriving all men of their civil and religious privileges, who will not receive the *mark* of

[x] See Barruel and Robison.

union

union with its abominable principles?—who has "made war with the faints," or fervants of God, and has "overcome many;" and who now openly blafphemes the God of heaven?

To what height of enormity—to what extent of dominion—the power of this tremendous image will be permitted to rife, muft remain for futurity to difcover.—But who will now fay it is impoffible, or even improbable, that the city of Rome fhould foon become the feat of *this* devaftating tyrant!—fhould foon become the feat of the Empire of APOSTATE INFIDELITY, or ATHEISM, as it has already been of PAGANISM, and POPERY; and thus render the refemblance between the image and the firft beaft yet more *literally* complete!—Nay, who will dare pronounce that this *moft dreadful* POWER of Antichrift, which has arifen in *the north*, fhall *not* "plant the taber-

tabernacles of his palaces between the feas, in the glorious holy mountain[z]?"

It is obfervable, that the *duration* of the moft *wonderful* form of the Papal Antichrift is fixed at 1260 years—from whatever time it obtained its power.— The *conquefts* of the Mahometan Antichrift were alfo determined to an exact point—but no limits feem to be fixed for the power or the duration of the power of the Infidel Antichrift—If the reafon of this diftinction be afked, it may perhaps be anfwered, Becaufe this was to be the *laft* form under which Antichrift fhould appear—" When the Son of man cometh, fhall he find *faith* on the earth?"—And, becaufe our Lord, who declares he will come " fuddenly and unexpectedly, as a thief in the night," will himfelf take exemplary vengeance

[z] Dan. xi. 45.

geance of this most daring and most bitter enemy to his name, his religion, and his servants—" If judgment begin at the house of God," alluding to the calamities of his chosen people the Jews, and the trials and corrections of the Christian Church, "what shall the end of *these wicked* be ?" It is expressly said that things " should be *hastened towards the end*, for the sake of the elect." The Mahometan and Papal Antichrists have been allowed to decline gradually before the time of their final destruction—but the *apostate Infidel* Antichrist may *perhaps*, I had almost said *probably*, be cut down when at the height of its conquest, and its glory, by some signal display of divine power—when the *whole* of Antichrist shall be destroyed—the ancient people of God " shall be. delivered[a]"—and the glorious kingdom of Christ shall be established, according to

[a] Dan. xii. 1.

the

the antient expectation of Jews and Christians, in peace, holinefs, and happinefs for ever.

I have thus endeavoured to explain fome of the various reafons which induce me to confider APOSTATE INFIDELITY, or ATHEISM, as one of the three principal forms of Antichrift by which the church of Chrift was to fuffer 1260 years—as having been defcribed by Prophecy exactly as it now appears in the world—as having appeared AS A POWER ACTING BY A DELEGATE exactly at the time it might have been expected to appear—as being the predicted fcourge of the corrupted church of Chrift, and the *laſt* form of power which its enemy will be permitted to affume.—In this Chapter I have nearly confined myfelf to the Prophecies of Daniel and of St. John, becaufe they contain the principal paffages which a fuperficial reader might imagine to be irreconcileable with the opinion which I

pre-

presume to offer, and with the interpretations of the best Commentators respecting the Church of Rome. And I trust it will now appear evident, that this opinion (supposing for a moment it be admitted as itself incontrovertibly just), arising out of EVENTS ACTUALLY PASSING BEFORE OUR EYES, which not only accurately fulfil "the word of Prophecy," but are utterly inexplicable without this key to point out their connexion with the past and future parts of the great plan which Prophecy displays—does in no respect contradict or invalidate the decided opinion of these learned men, that the Church of Rome is Antichrist.—Some of the most able and intelligent among these Commentators did indeed form nearly the same idea; and the accuracy of their conjectures concerning the *time* and the *country* wherein the power of Infidelity should *first* arise and reign, must be esteemed a strong

strong confirmation of its *truth* even to us who have been brought by the stream of time to scenes which lay beyond the limits of their sight.—I have only contended for a more *appropriate* application of *those parts* of the Prophecies which appeared to most of them difficult, incongruous, and of doubtful reference to the Papal power.—But while I consider this point as established by their labours beyond the possibility of injury, and the Prophecy respecting Mahometanism as having been immoveably fixed by proofs equally clear, I contend that APOSTATE INFIDELITY, and its delegated instrument, DEMOCRATIC TYRANNY, have been predicted with equal precision; and that POPERY, MAHOMETANISM, and INFIDELITY, are ALL parts of the same Antichristian Power, and subject to the same fate.

The following Chapters will shew the exactness

exactness with which the events of History correspond with the *received* interpretations concerning *Popery* and *Mahometanism*—trace the rise and progress of the Power of *Infidelity*, and point out the equal exactness with which it fulfils the Prophecies concerning it, with as much minuteness as the limits of this work will permit; and with a view to prove that these three branches of Antichristian Power form different parts of a general scheme of Prophecy.—And I trust it will be found, after an attentive examination, not only that this opinion is well founded, but that it shews the scattered rays of Prophetic light to be directed towards *one* point, gives harmony and connexion to the Apocalyptic visions, and explains the present fearful state of human affairs to be perfectly consistent with the Providence of God; and ultimately tending, under his direction, to the completion of the great,

UNVARYING PLAN OF HIM WHO "RULETH THE MADNESS OF THE PEOPLE," AND WHO MAKETH EVEN "THE WRATH OF MAN TO PRAISE HIM."

CLASS II.

CHAPTER THE FIRST.

THE RISE, PROGRESS, ESTABLISHMENT, AND DESTRUCTION OF THE PAPAL POWER OF ANTICHRIST.

AS this was the greateſt corruption of Chriſtianity that was to be permitted to take place in the world, it cannot be thought extraordinary, that more of the Prophecies, which we have brought forward to the notice of the Reader in the Introductory Chapter, are applicable to it, than to any other branch of Antichriſtian Power. As both Mahometaniſm and Infidelity confiſted more of open hoſtility, they were likely to be better

diſtin-

distinguished by Christians, without the aid of such strong prophetical light, as that which is afforded to expose, and to bring into full view, the counterfeit Christianity of the Church of Rome.

A combination of Prophecy with History will shew with what perfect exactness this Papal Power of Antichrist is marked out by the Prophets Daniel, St. Paul, and St. John.

To guide our enquiries to the right points of observation, St. John has designated, by certain appropriate allusions and descriptions, the *peculiar nature* of this power, the *time* when it began to manifest itself to the world, and the *seat* of its authority and government.

[a] *And I stood upon the sand of the sea, and saw a beast rise up out of the sea, hav-*

[a] Rev. xiii. 1.

ing

ing seven heads and ten horns, and upon his horns ten crowns, and upon his heads the name of blasphemy. ᵇThis wonderful beast with a crown on each horn, and a blasphemous inscription on each of his seven heads, denoted the new form of government that was to be erected in the city of Rome, by the great commotions of the world, after the Imperial Power had been destroyed, and the Empire was divided into ten distinct and independent sovereignties.

ᶜIn the mystical description which the Apostle afterwards gives of this beast, it will greatly assist our inquiries to discover by a given number, *when* this Antichristian power shall arise; and from thence ascertain with more precision what Power is meant by this prophetical representation. *Here is wisdom: let him*

ᵇ Lowman on the Revelations, p. 173.
ᶜ Lowman, p. 191.

I 3 *that*

*that hath underſtanding, count the number of the beaſt: for it is the number of a man, and his number is ſix hundred threeſcore and ſix*ᵈ. If we compute this number 666ᵉ from the time when St. John ſaw this Prophetic viſion, we ſhall find that this new Power was eſtabliſhed at the termination of this myſtic *number of years.* St. John was baniſhed to the iſle of Patmos in the latter part of the reign of Domitian, and returned from thence immediately on his death. Domitian reigned from 81 to 96. Now St. John ſaw the viſion in the iſle of Patmos; and it is generally acknowledged, that the Papacy received the temporal power, and became the beaſt, in 756.

ᵈ Rev. xiii. 18.

ᵉ It is very remarkable that this myſtic number ſhould ſo accurately apply both to the *time* when the Papal Antichriſt eſtabliſhed his reign, and the *titles* he aſſumed. See note to the Introductory Chapter, p. 129. Pyle's Paraphraſe, p. 105. Newton, vol. iii. p. 390. Lowman, p. 194.

The

The feat of this Power is fixed at Rome. THAT GREAT CITY, which in the times of Pagan idolatry had been the miftrefs of the antient world by the force of her arms, became in more modern ages, by the eftablifhment of her fpiritual laws, fo much exalted in power, as to *reign over the kings of the earth. The woman, upon whofe forehead was infcribed Myftery, Babylon the Great, the Mother of Harlots, and abominations of the earth, is,* according to the explanation of the angel, the city of Rome; for *the feven heads of the beaft that carried her are feven mountains on which the woman fitteth, and the woman which thou fawest is that great city, which reigneth over the kings of the earth.* Rome is well known to be built upon feven hills; and at the time when this révelation was communicated to St. John, its dominion was extended over all the known world[f].

Fur-

[f] "It feems intended by the angel's interpretation

Furnished with these plain directions by the Apostle, we proceed to trace the gradual rise and progress, decline and fall *of the Man of Sin*, as presented to our view by history and the course of present events.

No opportunity could be more favourable for the display of his ambition, his deceit, and his superstition, than the unhappy state of the Christian world in the fifth century. The members of the

tation that we should consider the city of Rome as marked out in this Prophecy for the seat of government to prevent mistakes, that we should not understand this Prophecy of an empire or government in any other place than the city of Rome, though it should take the name and style of the Roman Empire, as the Greek Emperors and the Emperors of Germany have severally done. This may give us a good reason why the city of Rome in this Prophecy is described by *its natural situation*, as well as by *its government*, and why *seven heads* are interpreted to mean *seven mountains*, as well as seven kings." Lowman, p. 177.

eastern

eaftern and the weftern churches were divided into parties, by religious difputes the moft unimportant; in confequence of which, they perfecuted each other with the greateft animofity and rancour. They were erroneous in faith, and degenerate in practice; and their credulity and ignorance fully prepared them for the reception of him, *whose coming was after the working of Satan, with all power, and signs, and lying wonders* [g].

His temporal dominion arofe out of the ruins of the Roman Empire. The change of the feat of government to Conftantinople, and the dethronement of Momyllus Auguftulus, were events that led immediately to the eftablifhment of a new Power. Auguftulus was depofed by Odoacer, King of the Heruli, in the year 476, who thus gave the

[g] 2 Theff. ii. 9.

deadly

deadly wound to the western Empire[h]. " This last Emperor of the West would be less entitled," says Gibbon[i], " than his

[h] Mosheim, vol. i. p. 228.
[i] Gibbon, vol. iii. p. 494. 4to. Edit. After the example of Mr. Whitaker in his excellent *View of the Prophecies*, I shall introduce into this and the following Chapter, several striking passages from *The Decline and Fall of the Roman Empire*, which show the completion of Prophecy. Gibbon has already rendered great service to this subject, as may be seen by referring to vol. i. c. 2. and he might contribute much more to it, did not the limits of my work confine me to particular quotations. Although as a disciple of Voltaire he delighted to asperse the characters of Christians, and represent every circumstance to their disadvantage; yet he was obliged as an Historian to listen to the voice of *truth*, and not to suppress important facts and events. His statements, even partial as they sometimes are, render him a powerful witness against Infidelity, by which he is manifestly actuated; and in favour of Christianity, which is so frequently the subject of his profane sarcasms. Not aware of the obvious use that may be made of his representations, like the idle servant in the parable of

his more immediate predeceffors to the notice of pofterity, if his reign, which was marked by the extinction of the Roman Empire in the Weft, *did not leave a memorable era in the hiftory of mankind.*"—Such was indeed the cafe, for thus *the beaft was wounded—he that letteth was taken out of the way*; and few obftacles remained to retard the full developement of *the Man of Sin*. Theodoric, the fucceffor of Auguftulus, by removing the feat of Empire to Ravenna, took from Rome all its dignity— her fenate and confuls were abolifhed, *and fhe was reduced to the level of the other cities of Italy.*

" [k] During a period of 200 years, Italy was unequally divided between the kingdom of the Lombards, and the ex-

---

of the talents; " he is condemned out of his own mouth."

[k] Gibbon, vol. iv. p. 443.

archate of Ravenna. The offices and proeffions, which the jealoufy of Conftantine had feparated, were united by the indulgence of Juftinian; and eighteen fucceffive Exarchs were invefted, in the decline of the Empire, with the full remains of civil, of military, and even of ecclefiaftical power. Their immediate jurifdiction, which was afterwards confecrated as the patrimony of St. Peter, extended over the modern Romagna, the marfhes or valleys of Ferrara and Commachio, five maritime cities, from Rimini to Ancona; and a fecond, inland Pentapolis, between the Adriatic coaft and the hills of the Apennine. Three fubordinate provinces of Rome, of Venice, and of Naples, which were divided by hoftile lands from the palace of Ravenna, acknowledged, both in peace and war, the fupremacy of the Exarch. The dutchy of Rome appears to have included the Tufcan, Sabine, and Latian conquefts, of the firft

400 years of the city; and the limits may be diſtinctly traced along the coaſt, from Civita Vecchia, to Terracina, and with the courſe of the Tyber from Ameria and Narni to the port of Oſtia."

"[1] Rome was oppreſſed by the iron ſceptre of the Exarchs, and a Greek, perhaps an eunuch, inſulted with impunity the ruins of the Capitol."....... " On the map of Italy, the meaſure of the exarchate occupies a very inadequate ſpace, but it included an ample proportion of wealth, induſtry, and population. The moſt faithful and valuable ſubjects eſcaped from the Barbarian yoke; and the banners of Pavia and Verona, of Milan and Padua, were diſplayed in their reſpective quarters, by the new inhabitants of Ravenna. The remainder of Italy was poſſeſſed by the Lombards."

[1] Gibbon, vol. iv. p. 444, 445.

" The

"ᵐ The Bishops of Italy and the adjacent islands acknowledged the Roman pontiff (Gregory the Great) as their special metropolitan. Even the existence, the union, or the translation of episcopal seats, was decided by his absolute discretion; and his successful inroads into the provinces of Greece, of Spain, and of Gaul, might countenance the more lofty pretensions of succeeding Popes."

"ⁿ In 728, Italy revolted from the eastern or Greek Emperor Leo; but the Popes exhorting the Italians not to separate from the body of the Roman monarchy, the Exarch was permitted to reside within the walls of Ravenna, a captive rather than a master: and till the imperial coronation of Charlemagne, the government of Rome and Italy was

ᵐ Gibbon, p. 459.
ⁿ Gibbon, vol. v. p. 111.

exer-

exercised in the name of the succeffors of Conftantine. The liberty of Rome, which had been oppreffed by the arms and arts of Auguftus, was refcued, after 750 years of fervitude, from the perfecution of Leo the Ifaurian. By the Cefars, the triumphs of the Confuls had been annihilated: in the decline and fall of the Empire, the God Terminus, the facred boundary, had infenfibly feceded from the Ocean, the Rhine, the Danube, and the Euphrates; and Rome was reduced to her antient territory from Viterbo to Terracina, and from Narni to the mouth of the Tyber."

" ° When the fovereignty of the Greek Emperors was extinguifhed, the ruins of Rome prefented the fad image of depopulation and decay: her flavery was an habit, her liberty an accident; the effect of fuperftition, and the object of her

° Gibbon, vol. v. p. 112.

own

own amazement and terror. The laſt veſtige of the ſubſtance, or even the forms, of the conſtitution, was obliterated from the practice and memory of the Romans; and they were devoid of knowledge, or virtue, again to build the fabric of a commonwealth. Their ſcanty remnant, the offspring of ſlaves and ſtrangers, was deſpicable in the eyes of the victorious Barbarians. As often as the Franks or Lombards expreſſed their moſt bitter contempt of a foe, they called him a Roman; 'and in this name,' ſays the Biſhop Liutprand, 'we include whatever is baſe, whatever is cowardly, whatever is perfidious, the extremes of avarice and luxury, and every vice that can proſtitute the dignity of human nature.' By the neceſſity of their ſituation, the inhabitants of Rome were caſt into the rough model of a republican government: they were compelled to elect ſome judges in peace and ſome leaders in war: the nobles aſſembled to

deli-

deliberate, and their refolves could not be executed without the union and confent of the multitude. *The ſtyle of the Roman ſenate and people was revived, but the ſpirit was fled; and their new independence was diſgraced by the tumultuous conflict of licentiouſneſs and oppreſſion.* The want of laws could only be fupplied by the influence of religion, and their foreign and domeftic counfels were moderated by the authority of the Bifhop. His alms, his fermons, his correfpondence with the kings and prelates of the Weft, his recent fervices, their gratitude, and oath, accuftomed the Romans to confider him as the firft magiftrate or prince of the city. The Chriftian humility of the popes was not offended by the name of *Dominus,* or Lord; and their face and infcription are ftill apparent on the moft ancient coins. Their temporal dominion is now confirmed by the reverence of a thoufand years; and their nobleft title

virtues, assumed the office of champion of the Roman Church."

When Astolphus began to make preparations for the conquest of Rome, " the terrified Pontiff[q], Stephen II. addresses himself to his powerful patron and protector, Pepin; represents to him his deplorable condition, and implores his assistance. *The French Monarch embarks with zeal in his cause, crosses the Alps A. D. 754. with a numerous army; and having defeated Astolphus, obliged him by a solemn treaty to deliver up to the see of Rome, the exarchate of Ravenna, Pentapolis, and all the cities, castles, and territories, which he had seized in the Roman dukedom.* It was not however long before the Lombard prince violated without remorse, an engagement which he had entered into with reluctance. In the year

[q] Mosheim, vol. i. p. 353.

755,

755, he laid fiege to Rome for the fecond time, but was again obliged to fue for peace, by the victorious arms of Pepin, who returned into Italy, and forcing *the Lombard to execute the treaty he had so audaciously violated*, made *a new grant* of the Exarchate, and of Pentapolis, to the Roman Pontiff and his fucceffors in the apoftolic See of St. Peter. *And thus was the Bishop of Rome raifed to the rank of a temporal Prince.*" 'The fplendid donation was granted in fupreme and abfolute dominion, *and the world beheld for the firft time a Chriftian Bishop invefted with the prerogatives of a temporal prince*; the choice of magiftrates, the exercife of juftice, the impofition of taxes, and the wealth of the palace of Ravenna........" Before the end of the eighth century fome apoftolical fcribe, perhaps the notorious Ifidore, compofed the Decretals, and the Do-

' Gibbon, c. 49. p. 124, 125, 126.

nation

nation of Conſtantine, the two magic pillars of the ſpiritual and temporal monarchy of the Popes. This memorable donation was introduced to the world, by an Epiſtle of Adrian the firſt, who exhorts Charlemagne to imitate the liberality, and revive the name of the great Conſtantine. According to the legend, the firſt of the Chriſtian Emperors was healed of the leproſy, and purified in the waters of baptiſm by St. Silveſter, the Roman Biſhop. His royal proſelyte withdrew from the ſeat and patrimony of St. Peter; declared his reſolution of founding a new capital in the Eaſt; and reſigned to the Popes the free and perpetual ſovereignty of Rome, Italy, and the provinces of the Weſt. This fiction was productive of the moſt beneficial effects. The Greek princes were convicted of the guilt of uſurpation; and the revolt of Gregory was the claim of his lawful inheritance. The ſovereignty of Rome no longer depended ed on the choice of a fickle people; and the *succeſſors of St. Peter and Conſtantine were inveſted with the purple and prerogatives of the Ceſars.*"

Thus did the myſtery[s] *of iniquity begin to work, with all deceivableneſs of unrighteouſneſs.* Thus was the ſovereign Pontiff *mighty in power*[t], *but not by his own power; and thus did he practiſe and proſper, and through his policy he cauſed craft to proſper in his hand.* Thus Rome[u] acquired a new ſeat and dominion in this patrimony of St. Peter, which has continued for above a thouſand years. The beaſt appeared to be wounded to death, —but the *deadly wound* inflicted by the ſword of Odoacer, King of the Heruli, was healed, after the Roman Empire had received ſuch an injury in *one of its heads*, or forms of government (that is,

[s] 2 Theſſ. ii. 7.   [t] Dan. viii. 24.
[u] Lowman, p. 198, 176.

the

the sixth) as left no probable prospect that Rome should ever more rise to power and empire. *And all the world wondered after the beast:* for this event of a new and extraordinary form of government, *divers from all others*—" this sacerdotal monarchy," as Gibbon calls it, excited the astonishment of mankind in the succeeding ages of its aggrandizement.

" [x] After their return from Avignon, the keys of St. Peter were guarded by the sword of St. Paul. Rome was commanded by an impregnable citadel: the use of cannon is a powerful engine against popular seditions: a regular force of cavalry and infantry was enlisted under the banners of the Pope: his ample revenues supplied the resources of war; and, from the extent of his domain, he could bring down on a rebellious city

[x] Gibbon, vol. vi. p. 613, 614.

an

an army of hostile neighbours and loyal subjects. Since the union of the dutchies of Ferrara and Urbino, the Ecclesiastical State extends from the Mediterranean to the Adriatic, and from the confines of Naples to the banks of the Po; and as early as the sixteenth century, the greater part of that spacious and fruitful country acknowledged the lawful claims and temporal sovereignty of the Roman Pontiffs. Their claims were readily deduced from the genuine or fabulous donations of the darker ages: the successive steps of their final settlement would engage us too far in the transactions of Italy, and even of Europe; the crimes of Alexander the sixth, the martial operations of Julius the second, and the liberal policy of Leo the tenth, a theme which has been adorned by the pens of the noblest historians of the times. In the first period of their conquests, till the expedition of Charles the eighth, the Popes might successfully wrestle wreftle with the adjacent princes and ftates, whofe military force was equal, or inferior, to their own."

Power was indeed given unto him over all kindreds, and tongues, and nations—for the Pope affumed the prerogative of being the fupreme fovereign of the Chriftian Church, and exercifed for many ages an uncontrolled and univerfal authority. *The kings gave their power and ftrength unto him,* as previous to the Reformation all the monarchs of the Weft acknowledged him as their fuperior and lord, and, as his vaffals, fubmitted to his power and his caprice. In the fifth century Pope Zechary I. depofed Childeric, King of France, the laft of the Merovingian race, and abfolved his fubjects from their oaths of allegiance[y]. In the eighth century,

[y] " Socrates faith of the Church of Rome and Alexandria, the moft famous Churches in the Apoftles' time, that about the year 430, the Roman and

tury, Paul I. excommunicated Conftantinus Copronymus, the Greek Emperor, becaufe he endeavoured to abolifh the worfhip of images. Henry IV. Emperor of Germany, was depofed and excommunicated in the eleventh century, by Pope Hildebrand II. " Under [z] that young and ambitious prieft, Innocent III. the fucceffors of St. Peter attained the full meridian of their greatnefs; and in a reign of eighteen years he exercifed a defpotic command over the Emperors and Kings, whom he raifed and depofed; over the nations, whom an interdict of months or years deprived, for the offence of their rulers, of the exercife of Chriftian worfhip.—In the Council of the Lateran, he acted as the ecclefiaftical, almoft as the temporal fovereign of the Eaft and Weft. It was

and Alexandrian Bifhops, leaving their facred functions, were degenerated to a fecular rule or dominion." Hooker's Eccl. Polity, p. 152.

[z] Gibbon, vol. vi. p. 109.

at the feet of his Legate that John, King of England, furrendered his crown; and Innocent may boaft of the two moft fignal triumphs over fenfe and humanity, the eftablifhment of tranfubftantiation [a], and the origin of the Inquifition. At his voice, two crufades, the fourth and the fifth, were undertaken."—[b] In the fame century, in which the fame hiftorian fays, that " Charles the Fourth received the gift or promife of the empire from the Roman Pontiff, who, in the exile or captivity of Avignon, affected the dominion of the earth," the Monkifh miffionaries kept the Papal banner flying in China; and Pope Benedict XII. received a folemn embaffy from the Khan of the Tartars. In the next age, Alexander IV. gave a rare fpecimen of Papal prefumption, in dividing Ame-

---

[a] About the year 931, Pafchafius Radbertus firft maintained the real prefence in the Sacrament.
[b] Whitaker, p. 241.

rica between the Portuguese and the Spaniards. "In the seventeenth century, Alphonso Mendez, the Catholic Patriarch of Ethiopia, accepted, in the name of Urban VIII. the homage of the Emperor of Abyssinia and his court—I confess, said the Emperor on his knees, that the Pope is the Vicar of Christ, the Successor of St. Peter, and the Sovereign of the world: to him I swear true obedience, and at his feet I offer my person and kingdom."

'And to shew the high prerogatives to which the Church of Rome holds itself intitled, we have only to appeal to their own writers for authentic proofs. Cardinal Bellarmine, when treating of the Roman Pontiffs, tells us that they must peculiarly well understand the authority of their own See. Let us there-

c Babylon in the Revelation of St. John, by Townson, p. 9.

fore hear them speak from their apostolical chair.

"He who reigneth on high, to whom all power is given in heaven and in earth; hath committed the one holy Catholic and Apostolical Church, out of which there is no salvation, to be governed with plenitude of power by one only, on earth; namely, by Peter the prince of the Apostles, and by the successor of Peter, the Roman Pontiff. *This one he hath constituted a prince over all nations, and all kingdoms; to pluck up, waste, destroy, plant, and build.*"

These are the words of Pope Pius V. in his Bull [d] against Queen Elizabeth; towards the conclusion of which, "Supported," he says, "by the authority of

[d] This Bull may be seen at length in Camden's Annals of Queen Elizabeth, under the year 1570, and in Burnet's Hist. of the Reformation, vol. ii. Collection of Records, p. 377.

him

him who hath seen fit to place him, however unequal to so great a charge, in this supreme throne of justice, he declares, in the plenitude of his Apostolical authority, the said Elizabeth laid under a sentence of Anathema, deprived of all right and title to her kingdom, her subjects absolved from all oaths of allegiance to her, and those who obey her, involved in the like sentence of Anathema."

The See of Rome, as it was rising to this plenitude of power, endeavoured to support itself by every appeal to the peculiar favour of heaven. Many of the Popes confirmed their authority by the pretended evidence of ghosts, and of persons affirmed to be risen from the dead.—Such is the exact conduct of him who was predicted *to come after the working of Satan, with all power, and signs, and lying wonders, and with all deceivableness of unrighteousness, who deceiv-*

eth them that dwell in the earth, by means of those miracles which he had power to do. The Papal See has laid claim to the power of working miracles, as to one of the marks of the true church, and persuaded the credulous and the superstitious of the dark ages, to allow its pretensions. The history of Italy, France, Spain, and Portugal, more especially—countries the most devoted to the interests of the sovereign Pontiffs—can abundantly prove the frequency and the extent of pious frauds. The Legends of the Romish saints are filled with accounts of miracles reported to have been wrought for the establishment of corrupt doctrines, and idolatrous worship.

" It is observable[e], that the Man of Sin is said to perform his miracles, *in the sight of men* in order to deceive them, and *in the sight of the beast* in order to

[e] Newton, vol. iii. p. 236, 237.

serve him: but not *in the sight of God* to serve his cause, or promote his religion. Now miracles, visions, and revelations, are the mighty boast of the church of Rome; the contrivances of an artful cunning clergy, to impose upon an ignorant credulous laity. Even *fire* is pretended to *come down from heaven*, as in the case of St. Anthony's fire, and other instances cited by Brightman[f], and other writers on the Revelation; and in solemn excommunications, which are called the *thunders* of the church, and are performed with the ceremony of casting down burning torches from on high, as symbols and emblems of *fire from heaven*. Miracles are thought so necessary and essential, that they are reckoned among the notes of the Catholic Church; and they are alleged principally in support of purgatory, prayers for the dead, the worship of saints, images, and relics, and

[f] Vide Brightman. et Poli Synops. in locum.

the like (as they are called) Catholic doctrines. But if these miracles were all *real*, we learn from hence what opinion we ought to frame of them; and what then shall we say, if they are all *fictions* and *counterfeits?* They are indeed so far from being any proof of the true church, that they are rather a proof of a false one;—they are, as we see, the distinguishing mark of Antichrist."

To corroborate these observations, let us turn to the description of the church in the tenth century[g]. " Both Greeks and Latins placed the essence and life of religion in the worship of images[h] and departed saints, in searching after with zeal, and preserving with a devout care and veneration, the sacred relics of holy men and women; and in accumulating

---

[g] Mosheim, vol. i. p. 456.
[h] The worship of images was established at the second Council of Nice, A. D. 787. See Lowman, p. 206.

riches upon the Priests and Monks, whose opulence increased with the progress of superstition. Scarcely did any Christian dare to approach the throne of God, without rendering first the saints and images propitious by a solemn round of expiatory rites and lustrations.—The fears of purgatory, of that fire which was to destroy the remaining impurities of departed souls, were now carried to the greatest height, and exceeded by far the terrifying apprehensions of infernal torments; for they hoped to avoid the latter easily, by dying enriched with the prayers of the clergy, or covered with the merits and mediations of the saints; while from the pains of purgatory they knew there was no exemption. The clergy therefore, finding these superstitious terrors admirably adapted to increase their authority and promote their interest, used every method to augment them, and by the most pathetic discourses,

courses, accompanied with monstrous fables, and fictitious miracles, they laboured to establish the doctrine of purgatory, and also to make it appear that they had a mighty interest in that formidable region."

The sovereign Pontiff exercised the authority he had obtained in making and publishing edicts and constitutions for the establishment of idolatry. Divine honours were conferred upon reputed saints, who were solemnly canonized according to regular forms of consecration. As they were supposed to be possessed of divine power, the most fervent prayers were offered up to them—*the name of God, and of them that dwell in heaven, was blasphemed*, and the Supreme Being was deprived of the glory and worship due to him alone, and the name of the genuine saints and angels was abused by setting them up as mediators and intercessors

cessors for mankind. *The divine laws were changed*[i]. In the Popish mass-books, and in the tables written in the churches, the second commandment, so directly pointed against all idolatry, was omitted; and, in order to make up the complete number of the Decalogue, the tenth commandment is divided into two. It has been the practice of the Church of Rome for many ages, to dispense for money with the due observance of the precepts of the Gospel, and to sell indulgences, pardons, and absolutions, even for crimes of the most atrocious nature[k]. Of the progress of this infamous traffick, we may judge by the account given of it in the twelfth century.

[i] Dan. vii. 25.

[k] I refer the Reader to the Catalogue of Indulgences printed in 1514, and quoted by Simpson in his Key to the Prophecies, p. 247.

" When

"[1] When the Roman Pontiffs caft an eye upon the immenfe treafures, that the inferior rulers of the church were accumulating by the fale of indulgences, they thought proper to limit the power of the Bifhops in remitting the penalties impofed upon tranfgreffors, and affumed almoft entirely this profitable traffick to themfelves. In confequence of this new meafure, the court of Rome became the general magazine of indulgences: and the Pontiffs, when either the wants of the Church, the emptinefs of their coffers, or the demon of avarice prompted them to look out for new fubfidies, publifhed not only an univerfal, but alfo a complete, or what they called, a plenary remiffion of all the temporal pains and penalties, which the Church had annexed to certain tranfgreffions. They

---

[1] Mofheim, vol. i. p. 595. See likewife p. 596, and 723.

went still farther; and not only remitted the penalties which the civil and ecclefiastical laws had enacted againſt tranſgreſſors, *but audaciouſly uſurped the authority which belongs to God alone, and impiouſly pretended to aboliſh even the puniſhments which are reſerved in a future ſtate for the workers of iniquity*; a ſtep this, which the Biſhops with all their avarice and preſumption had never once ventured to take." *He opened his mouth in blaſphemy againſt God.* "God alone hath power to forgive ſins," is the declaration of our Lord.

"[m] When a new Pope is inaugurated, he is clothed with the pontifical robes, and crowned, and placed upon the altar of the church of St. Peter at Rome, and the Cardinals come and kiſs his feet, which ceremony is called *adoration*. They firſt elect, and then they worſhip him;

[m] Newton, vol. iii. p. 240.

as in the medals of Martin V. where two are reprefented crowning the Pope, and two kneeling before him with this infcription, *Quem creant, adorant*—whom they create, they adore." Can any one be a fpectator of this impious ceremony, and not be ftruck by the appearance of the *Man of Sin who exalteth himfelf, and as God fitteth in the temple of God, fhowing himfelf that he is God?*

"[n] Among the Catholics, Cardinal Orfi fays, there is no one who dares deny, or can deny, that Jefus Chrift has inftituted a monarchy, or form of monarchical government in his church, and that the fupreme head of this monarchy is the Roman Pontiff." This is declared with great folemnity from the portico of St. Peter's Church, in the prefence of a numerous affembly at the coronation of a Pope; when a Cardinal Deacon hav-

[n] Townfon's Babylon, p. 11.

ing taken the mitre from his head, another places on it the triple crown, and fays, "Receive this Tiara adorned with three crowns; and know that thou art Father of Princes and Kings, *Governor of the Globe of the Earth*, Vicegerent of our Saviour Jefus Chrift."

With fuch pretenfions to more than mortal honours, agrees the language of Gregory II. addreffed in his Epiftle to the Emperor Leo, in the eighth century, which will fhow *how foon* the fovereign Pontiff began *to exalt himfelf*, even when affecting a ftyle of humility—"° Are you ignorant that the Popes are the bond of union, the mediators of peace, between the Eaft and the Weft? The eyes of the nations are fixed on our humility; *and they revere as a God upon earth*, the Apoftle St. Peter, whofe image you threaten to de-

° Gibbon, vol. v. p. 107.

ftroy.

ſtroy. The remote and interior kingdoms of the Weſt preſent their homage to Chriſt *and his Vicegerent.*" Similar were the preſumptuous, or rather blaſphemous appellations either claimed or approved by his ſucceſſors. Innocent III. aſſerted that the Popes held on earth the place not of mere men, but of the true God. Martin V. in the inſtructions which he gave to the ambaſſadors whom he ſent to Conſtantinople, ſtyled himſelf the *Moſt Holy* and the *Moſt Bleſſed*, who has the celeſtial empire, who is Lord upon Earth, Succeſſor of St. Peter, the Chriſt of the Lord, the Maſter of the Univerſe, the Father of Kings, and the light of the world. An Archbiſhop thus addreſſed Leo X. " All power is given unto you, and he who ſaid *all*, excepted nothing." This Pope ſuffered himſelf to be ſtyled Divine Majeſty. Paul V. allowed himſelf to be called Vice-God, and received the prophetic language of Jeremiah and Daniel as applicable to himself[p]. Thus the authority with which for many centuries the Popes claimed the difpofal of the dominion of the earth, the obedience which they required to their decrees, and the exalted and impious titles which they affumed or authorized, demonftrate the full eftablifhment of the predicted univerfal empire. Modern like antient Rome kept the world in fubjection to its laws: *it devoured, brake in pieces, and ftamped the refidue with its feet.*

But where, it may be afked, are any traces to be found in the Prophecies, of thofe peculiar inftitutions and practices which have diftinguifhed the Church of Rome fo very remarkably from all others —*the Celibacy of her clergy*—*the inftitution of her Fafts*—*and the fpirit of Perfecution*, that has fo often drawn the fword againft the more pure profeffors of the Gofpel?

[p] Jerem. xxvii. 8. Dan. vii. 14.

q Now the Spirit speaketh expressly, that in the latter times some shall depart from the faith, FORBIDDING TO MARRY, AND COMMANDING TO ABSTAIN FROM MEATS, *which God hath created to be received with thanksgiving of them which believe and know the truth.*

Had the great Apostle of the Gentiles beheld, in the ages that succeeded his own, the sects of *Encratites,* and *Apostolici*^r, who observed the most rigid abstinence, and condemned marriage as an unholy state—Had he seen the numerous monks, who, forming the different classes of *Cœnobites* and *Anachorets,*^s, devoted themselves to a recluse life, and gradually overflowed like a torrent, first the Greek, and afterwards the Latin Church—And if he had lived to

---

q 1 Tim. iv. 1, 3.
r Mosheim, vol. i. p. 619.
s Gibbon, vol. iii. p. 523.

see all Europe covered with religious houses[t], and those houses peopled with nuns and friars of all denominations, who, in common with the Popish laity, preserved during Lent, and at other times, the injunctions of the sovereign Pontiff, to abstain from flesh—The great Apostle might have drawn a more full picture; but he could not have given a more striking sketch by a few masterly strokes, than he has done[u].

" We learn[x] from Mosheim, that the great work ascribed to the monastic orders, the support of the Papal authority, was more especially performed by two mendicant classes of Monks, who might well be termed the two horns of the

[t] Mosheim, vol. ii. p. 9.
[u] The Prophecy concerning the establishment of the *monastic orders*, strikes with the greater force, when we recollect that those orders were the great supports of the Papal authority.
[x] Whitaker, p. 226.

beast.

beaft. 'The power of the Dominicans and Francifcans furpaffed greatly that of the other two orders, and rendered them fingularly confpicuous in the eyes of the world. During three centuries thefe two fraternities governed, with an almoft univerfal and abfolute fway, both ftate and church, filled the moft eminent pofts ecclefiaftical and civil, taught in the univerfities and churches with an authority, before which all oppofition was filent, and maintained the pretended Majefty of the Roman Pontiffs, againft Kings, Princes, Bifhops, and Heretics, with incredible ardour, and equal fuccefs.' And fince the Reformation, the Papal pretenfions to univerfal fupremacy have been fupported with equal zeal, and even carried into another hemifphere, by that order who have affumed the very name of Jefus."

The fpirit of perfecution is acknow-

y Mofheim, vol. ii. p. 656. 4to. Edit.

ledged

ledged to be one of the leading marks of Antichrift. Daniel fays, that "the king," *who was divers from all others, fhall wear out the faints of the moft High.* In like manner, the beaft in the Revelation of St. John *deftroys the faints of the moft High—It was given to him to make war with the faints, and to overcome them—The woman that reprefents Papal Rome is drunk with the blood of the faints.* How applicable are thefe defcriptions to the conduct of the Papifts in various ages! It has been computed that fifty millions of Proteftants have at different times been the victims of their perfecutions, and been cruelly put to death on account of their religious opinions[z]. But for *particular* inftances of the completion of thefe Prophecies, we look no farther into the bloody annals of the Church of Rome, than to the cruelties exercifed

[z] Simpfon, p. 346.

againft

against the Albigenses and Waldenses[a]—the tortures and deaths of the martyrs in our own country, in the reign of Philip and Mary[b]—the barbarities exercised upon the innocent natives of South America—*the acts of faith* performed in Spain and Portugal—the dark and sanguinary proceedings of the Inquisition[c]

[a] Gibbon, c. liv. p. 535. Lowman, p. 208.

[b] The law for burning heretics in England was first passed in the reign of Henry IV. It was not repealed till the year 1677. Simpson, p. 345.

[c] The Inquisition was established A. D. 1209. Dominick was made first Inquisitor by Pope Innocent III. This *holy* office, in the style of the Roman court, has improved the methods of persecution, far beyond what was known in the days of antient Babylon and Rome, and has long been the most dreadful and barbarous tribunal the world ever saw, for all ensnaring arts of injustice in prosecution, all inhuman severity and cruelty in punishment: as is evidently proved at large in Limborch's History of the Inquisition. Lowman, p. 201, 202.

—the

—the revocation of the Edict of Nantz, and the maffacre of St. Bartholomew. Thefe facts alone are fufficient to fhew, that in this vindictive and perfecuting Church was found *the blood of prophets and faints, and of all that were flain upon the earth.*

"^d The countries that have been moft cruelly harraffed, and deluged with Proteftant blood, are Spain, Portugal, Poland, Hungary, Bohemia, Italy, Germany, England, Scotland, Ireland, Flanders, Holland, Savoy, Piedmont, and France. France, indeed, has exceeded all the nations in Europe for acts of perfecution, blood, and cruelty. Perfecution for confcience fake began there early, and continued long. Even fo late as the beginning of the prefent century, the Proteftants endured there as much as any people ever did fince the begin-

---

^d Simpfon, p. 348, 349, 350, 351, 352, 353.

ning

ning of the world. Savoy, Piedmont, and Hungary, have suffered much; but France boasts of more martyrs to the truth than any other kingdom in Europe. We think, and we think justly, that the late massacres in that distracted nation are very dreadful: but what are they, when compared with what the Protestants underwent upon several occasions? At one time, by order of the king, bishops, and priests, thirty thousand (some say sixty thousand) Protestants were murdered in the course of a few days. This shocking business was executed about two hundred years ago. After this a civil war broke out between the Papists and Protestants, which continued to rage near sixty years in the very heart of the country, in which Puffendorf assures us [e], 'there were destroyed a million of people. One hun-

---

[e] Introduction to the History of Europe, c. 5. p. 201.

dred

dred and fifty millions of money were spent. Nine cities, four hundred villages, twenty thousand churches, two thousand monasteries, and ten thousand houses, were burnt or laid level with the ground.'—This is but a little more than one hundred and fifty years ago."

" And then again in the reign of Louis the Fourteenth, about an hundred years since, that haughty monarch began another persecution against the Protestants, during the course of which an innumerable multitude of people were harrassed and put to death in the most cruel and ignominious manner men or devils could invent: and eight hundred thousand persons (Voltaire says five hundred thousand) left the kingdom, and fled into other countries, whithersoever they could escape the safest and most expeditiously."

" *All these things were transacted in France.*

France. The Pope of Rome, as head of the church, was at the bottom of the whole. The archbishops, bishops, and clergy, very generally, concurred; and many of them even marched at the head of the king's troops with small crucifixes in their hands, exhorting the people to turn and embrace their superstitious and idolatrous nonsense, or commanding the soldiers to execute the law upon them. The king, the parliament, the princes, the nobles, the gentry, and the people of the country, all concurred in the diabolical measures. And when the thirty, or sixty thousand Protestants before mentioned, were massacred, we are particularly informed, that the Pope, as soon as he received the news, appointed public thanksgiving, and Te Deum was sung for joy in the church of St. Louis. He, moreover, published a bull of pardons, and extraordinary indulgences to such as should pray for the heavenly assistance to the king and kingdom of France for rooting

ing out heretics. The king, archbishops, bishops, clergy, and nobles too, went in public procession, singing the praises of God for this bloody and diabolical transaction."

And yet whilst the *Man of Sin* was thus *exalting himself*, and pursuing his career of ambition and persecution, the Providence of God raised up witnesses of the truth in every age, who in a publick manner testified against the general corruptions of the church, its idolatrous doctrines, and superstitious practices [f]. *The patience and the faith of the saints* were to be conspicuous during the whole time that *the witnesses prophesied in sackcloth*—for neither the menaces nor the punishments of the Church of Rome abated their courage, or extinguished their zeal. In the tenth and eleventh centuries, Claude Clement Bishop of

[f] Lowman, p. 207.

Turin,

Turin, Ratramne a Monk of Corbie, John Scott, and Berenger, who was favoured by Bifhop Bruno, oppofed the worfhip of images, and the doctrine of the real prefence of Chrift in the Sacrament [g]. Peter Fitz Caffiodor, Michael Cæfenas, William Occam, and Marfilius a celebrated lawyer of Padua, expofed the various herefies and errors of the Church of Rome, its pride, avarice, tyranny, and exactions. Du Pin obferves, whofe teftimony is the more remarkable as he is a Popifh Hiftorian[h], " that in the twelfth age there were many hereticks in many places, who openly attacked the facraments of the church, and defpifed her moft holy ceremonies: that the feverity, with which they who were taken were punifhed, did not hinder the fect from increafing: that their doctrines fpread through all

[g] Newton, vol. iii. p. 182.
[h] Lowman, p. 208.

the

the kingdom of France: many heretics appeared, whofe chief view was to diffuade men from communion with the church in its facraments, and to overturn its hierarchy, order, and difcipline."

The thirteenth century was more particularly diftinguifhed by the victory gained over the fuperftitions of the Church of Rome, by the Waldenfes and Albigenfes. "[i] Driven from their own country on account of their religious opinions, they fled for refuge into foreign lands, fome into Germany, and fome into Britain. [k] Pope Innocent III. determined to put a ftop to their zealous exertions; and he not only appointed his Legates to preach againft them,

---

[i] Newton, vol. iii. p. 183. For an account of their *particular opinions* fee the teftimonies of their *enemies*, quoted by Lowman, p. 211. See likewife Gibbon, c. liv. p. 535.

[k] Lowman, p. 208.

but excited the secular princes and the common people to destroy them. He published a Croisade against them, which occasioned a long war between Montfort, General of the Cross-Bearers, and the Count of Thouloufe, in which much blood was spilt, and many lives were sacrificed[1]. But notwithstanding the rage of *the Man of Sin* so furiously directed against them, they grew and multiplied so fast in Germany that at the beginning of the thirteenth century, it is computed that there were 80,000 of them in Bohemia, Austria, and the neighbouring territories, and they pertinaciously defended their doctrines even unto death." In the fourteenth century John Wickliff[m], a man of distinguished reputation in the University of Oxford, began in England to oppose the authority of the Pope, as well as

[1] Newton, vol. iii. p. 184.
[m] Newton, vol. iii. p. 184.

many of his corruptions and errors. A‑
mong his moſt eminent followers were
John Huſs, and Jerom of Prague, per‑
ſons of great conſideration in the Uni‑
verſity of that place—William Sawtre,
pariſh prieſt of St. Oſith, in London—
Thomas Badby, and Sir John Oldcaſtle.
Theſe all ſuffered death as heretics.—In
them was manifeſt "*the patience of the
ſaints: here are they that kept the com‑
mandments of God, and the faith of Jeſus.*

°The number of theſe faithful wit‑
neſſes ͬ continued to increaſe, although
every engine of oppreſſion and perſecu‑
cution was raiſed againſt them; for it
was granted to the beaſt for a certain ap‑

ⁿ Rev. xiv. 12.
° Lowman, p. 212. For a more particular ac‑
count of the actions and ſufferings of theſe wit‑
neſſes, or martyrs, ſee Flaccius Illyricus, the Cen‑
turiators of Magdeburg, Uſher, Allix, Spanheim,
and other authors.
ᵖ Newton, vol. iii. p. 197.

pointed

pointed time, *to make war with the faints and to overcome them*; and even to be *drunk with the blood of the faints.* They arose in every age of the church, and appeared in almost every country; more particularly in Italy, France, Spain, England, Germany, and Bohemia. The many thousands that were destroyed by the armies brought against them, and by the Inquisition, are sufficient evidences of their great numbers. They boldly protested against the corruptions of the Church of Rome, and, having witnessed a good confession of the true faith, fell victims to her bloody spirit of persecution. "[q] The assemblies of the Paulicians, or Albigeois, were extirpated by fire and sword, and the bleeding remnant escaped by flight, concealment, or Catholic conformity. *But the invincible spirit which they kindled still lived and breathed in the western world.* In

[q] Gibbon, vol. v. c. 54.

the ſtate, in the church, and even in the cloiſter, a latent ſucceſſion was preſerved of the diſciples of St. Paul; *who proteſted againſt the tyranny of Rome, embraced the Bible as the rule of faith*, and purified their creed from all the viſions of the Gnoſtic theology. The ſtruggles of Wickliff in England, of Huſs in Bohemia, were premature and ineffectual; but the names of Zuinglius, Luther, and Calvin are pronounced with gratitude, as the deliverers of nations."

The courſe of Hiſtory and of Prophecy carries us forward to that auſpicious period, when the Proteſtants rejected the errors of the See of Rome, aſſerted the rights of conſcience, and reſtored the purity of the primitive church. Martin Luther in the year 1517, preached publickly in the church of Magdeburg, againſt the Indulgences granted by the ſovereign Pontiff; and by this magnanimous act began the re-

formation

formation of religion. *Then did Babylon the great fall from the height of her dominion*—Then were the faithful followers of the Lamb animated with new zeal by the fuccefs of the firft Reformers, and the voice from heaven was obeyed with alacrity, which faid, [r] COME OUT OF HER, MY PEOPLE, THAT YE BE NOT PARTAKERS OF HER SINS, AND THAT YE RECEIVE NOT OF HER PLAGUES.

With the fublime account given by St. John, of the choir of the bleffed fpirits chanting a new fong to celebrate the revival of primitive Chriftianity, this new epoch of Prophecy commences. " Daniel had been informed[s] concerning this power, whofe *look was more ftout than his fellows, that the judgment fhould fit, and they fhould take away his dominion, to confume and to deftroy it unto the*

[r] Rev. xiv. 1, &c.
[s] Whitaker, p. 249, 250, 251, 252.

end.

end. And St. Paul in the terms, *that wicked one whom the Lord shall consume with the spirit of his mouth, and destroy with the brightness of his coming*, characterizes that gradual decline from the plenitude of his power, through the prevalence of the word of the Lord, intimated before by the Prophet, and more fully prefigured by St. John in the predictions of three several steps, by which the authority of Rome should be lowered among men. *And I saw another angel fly in the midst of heaven, having the everlasting Gospel to preach unto them that dwell on the earth, and to every nation, and kindred, and tongue, and people, saying with a loud voice, Fear God, and give glory to him; for the hour of his judgment is come: and worship him that made heaven, and earth, and the sea, and the fountains of waters.* While the proclamation here made, that the hour of God's judgment is come, is well calculated to turn our thoughts to the

the fate of that power whose dominion it was declared to Daniel, should then begin to be consumed, an attentive Reader may discern, on perusing this passage, a certain degree of abruptness in the introduction of this symbol of the angel. From a choir of those who have been redeemed through the Gospel to a fresh publication of it, seems a rapid transition; yet most precisely does this mark the mode in which the Reformation began. For to that event (which was in fact a republication of the Gospel, and was so termed in a History of its progress, quoted by Mosheim, *Historia Evangelii Renovati*) every circumstance of this particular prediction is suited, and pointedly to this purpose are the words of the ecclesiastical Historian above mentioned, "while the Roman Pontiff slumbered in security at the head of the church, and saw nothing through-

---

[1] Mosheim, cent. 16. sect. 1. ch. 2.

out

out the vaſt extent of his dominion but tranquillity and ſubmiſſion; and while the worthy and pious profeſſors of genuine Chriſtianity almoſt deſpaired of ſeeing that Reformation on which their moſt ardent deſires and expectations were bent; an obſcure and inconſiderable perſon aroſe *on a ſudden*, in the year fifteen hundred and ſeventeen, and laid the foundation of this long expected change, by oppoſing, with undaunted reſolution, his ſingle force to the torrent of Papal ambition and deſpotiſm.' How juſtly does the latter part of this remark correſpond with the emblem of the text! Luther, ſays the Hiſtorian, laid the foundation of this long expected change: and this angel, the Apoſtle tells us, was ſeen to fly in the midſt of heaven. Contrary to the general fate of the preachers of new tenets, it was Luther's lot to proclaim his doctrine in the midſt of the figurative heavens;

heavens; before the Emperor and the Princes of the Empire affembled in open Diet. Patronized from the firft by Princes, the Reformation was introduced into the countries where it took place, by the authority of the fovereigns themfelves; not by a party firft gained among the fubjects, too powerful for the fovereign to refift. This emblematick meffenger of God had too the everlafting Gofpel; the Gofpel, of which it is the fundamental doctrine, that there is one God, and one Mediator between God and man: this he preached unto them that dwell on the earth, faying with a loud voice, FEAR GOD, AND GIVE GLORY TO HIM. Luther, we are told, when the famous indulgences of Leo X. were proclaimed in Germany, ' raifed his warning voice,' and in ninety-five propofitions, maintained publickly at Wittemberg, plainly pointed out the Roman Pontiff as a partaker in the guilt

of

of those who sold them, since he suffered the people to be seduced by such delusions, from placing their principal confidence in Christ, the only proper object of their trust.

" Again, as the angel called on men to worship Him who made heaven and earth; so after the appearance of an especial edict of Leo the tenth, in which that Pope commanded his spiritual subjects to acknowledge his power *of delivering* (I almost shudder at the blasphemy while I transcribe it) *from all the punishments due to sin and transgressions of every kind*; Luther published a German translation of the Bible, 'the different parts of which being successively and gradually spread abroad among the people, produced,' says Mosheim, ' a sudden and almost incredible effect, and extirpated root and branch the erroneous principles and superstitious doctrines

trines of the Church of Rome from the minds of a prodigious number of persons,' with such precision did the symbol mark its antitype, by the angel having in his hand the everlasting Gospel. And if the Reader wishes to see how rapidly the Reformation spread among the kindreds, tongues, and nations, he will find very satisfactory information in the work above quoted. Wherein too he will discover the commencement of a literal accomplishment of the words of Daniel *to take away his dominion*, in several sovereigns entirely withdrawing their realms from under the ecclesiastical jurisdiction of the Roman Pontiff."

Ever since the time of the Reformation, the Church of Rome has gradually been losing its antient splendor and greatness. The profound reverence in which her Governor was held, and the implicit obedience which was paid to his

his commands, are now confined to very narrow limits. The kingdoms which still acknowledge her jurisdiction have long set bounds to her avarice and ambition. The power of superstition and of delusion, by which her influence was supported over the minds of mankind, is overcome by the exertions of reason, and the light of pure and undefiled religion. Every attack that has been made by the pretended philosophers, or avowed infidels of France and Germany, has been aimed at Popery, as the *first* object of their hostility. The last twenty years include a number of events the most adverse to the interests of the Church of Rome. The order of the Jesuits, its most firm and able supporters, has been suppressed; and the inability of the sovereign Pontiff to prevent the execution of a measure so destructive to his authority, was proved by his ineffectual and degrading personal application to the Emperor Joseph. The monasteries of Germany, once filled with his most zealous adherents, are diffolved. Even Spain, once the moſt ſuperſtitious country in Europe, has abridged the powers of its Inquiſition, and pays with reluctance her accuſtomed tribute to the Head of the Church. The French, ſince the era of the Revolution, have buried the Catholic altar under the ruins of the Monarchical throne.

The memorable events even of the paſſing year have accelerated her decline. The French armies have ravaged Italy, and poured their fury upon *the ſeat of the beaſt*. Rome itſelf is become a prey to its Apoſtate and Infidel conquerors. The *temporal authority* of the Pope is *completely ſubverted*, and the ſemblance of the *antient Roman government is eſtabliſhed at Rome*, by the Democratic tyranny which reigns triumphant in its place. The Pope himſelf, after being expoſed to repeated inſults, fults, is degraded and driven from his throne; he is divefted of his honours and his ftate—ftripped of his poffeffions and revenues, and reduced to the abject condition of a wanderer, and an exile. Germany, Naples, Portugal, and Spain, view his degradation with indifference, if not with approbation; and France, the country of Pepin and of Charlemagne, the great founders of the Papal glory, is the inftrument of his overthrow, and enriches herfelf with his fpoils.

And if fuch are the *manifeft proofs* of the decline of the the Man of Sin from the height of his power, it may be afked, if there are any *correfpondent intimations of fuch events* to be found in the Holy Scriptures?

I adopt the words of Bifhop Newton[u], as containing the beft anfwer to

[u] Newton, vol. iii. p. 400.

this queftion. " The Prophets are not more expreffive of the elevation, than they are of the deftruction, of the Papal Antichrift. They not only predict his downfall in general terms, but alfo defcribe the manner and circumftances of it; and St. John's account being larger and more circumftantial and particular, will be the beft comment and explanation of the others."

And the ten horns which thou faweft upon the beaft, thefe fhall hate the whore, and fhall make her defolate and naked, and fhall eat her flefh, and fhall burn her with fire. For God hath put in their hearts, to fulfil his will, and to agree, and give their kingdom unto the beaft, until the words of God fhall be fulfilled. And the woman which thou faweft, is that great city, which reigneth over the kings of the earth.

To this Prophecy, the completion of which is fo manifeftly going on ftep by ftep step before our eyes, I subjoin the observations of Daubuz[x], and of Bishop Newton[y], the former published 78, and the latter more than 32 years ago; and I am the more particularly desirous of recommending them to the attention of the Reader, because they furnish him with proofs of the proper application of this prediction, and because they display the true principles of interpretation upon which these sagacious expositors of Prophecy have proceeded.

"As to the word *shall hate*, it implies, *shall forsake*; and if the kings in Christendom forsake Rome, what can follow, but that either they will combine to destroy it, or else rather stand by neuters, whilst some one of them performs this last office to destroy it?....The beast as such, the false prophet, and the whore,

---
[x] Daubuz's Commentary on the Revelations, p. 795, 796, 797. fol. 1720.
[y] Newton, vol. iii. p. 308. 3d Edit. 1766.

are

are inseparable companions, that is, the Romish Church or City, Popery, and Tyranny. But the horns shall-be separated from the whore, and consequently from the beast, or the exercise of that tyrannical power which makes them a beast, and maintains this whore in splendor and power. From this place and the following we *may safely conjecture, that the instruments God shall make use of to destroy Rome, not being said to come out of the Temple, shall not therefore be of the number of the true worshippers, or Protestants, but of those that are still horns upon the beast; that is, of such as are still in communion with Rome, at least some one or more of them.*"

And shall eat her flesh. Flesh, in the symbolical language, signifies the riches, goods, and possessions, of any person or subject conquered, oppressed, or slain..... By this third act of the horns, it appears that the secular powers, who shall attack this

this whore, will not only ftrip her of her riches and revenues, but alfo appropriate them to themfelves."

" *The ten horns fhall hate the whore*[z]; that is, by a common figure of the whole for a part, *fome* of the ten kings who formerly loved her, grown fenfible of her exorbitant exactions and oppreffions, *fhall hate her*, fhall ftrip and expofe, and plunder her, and utterly confume her with fire. Rome therefore will finally be deftroyed by fome of the princes, who are reformed, or fhall be reformed from Popery: *and as the kings of France have contributed greatly to her advancement, it is not impoffible, nor improbable, that fome time or other they may alfo be, the principal authors of her deftruction.* France hath already fhown fome tendency towards a reformation, and therefore may appear more likely to

[z] Newton, vol. iii. p. 308.

effect such a Revolution. *Such a revolution may reasonably be expected*, because this infatuation of Popish princes is *permitted* by divine Providence only for a certain period, *until the words of God shall be fulfilled,* and particularly the words of the Prophet Daniel—*They shall be given into his hand, until a time, and times, and the dividing of time :* but then, as it immediately follows, *the judgment shall sit, and they shall take away his dominion, to consume and to destroy it unto the end.*"

The observations of Bishop Newton are more definite with respect to the *Power*, which he expected would effect the subversion of the Papal greatness; but he expected also (and some other Commentators have agreed with him) that a *Reformation* would *previously* take place in France—but for this opinion he assigns no reason drawn from Scripture; whereas the opinion of Daubuz, that

that the inſtrument God would make uſe of, could not be true worſhippers, or Pro-teſtants, being *founded* on the *Prophecy itſelf,* has been *verified* by the events.

This apoſtaſy of thoſe who raiſed the power of Antichriſtian Rome, this degradation of her ſovereign Pontiff, whom the nations and kings of the earth once worſhipped, or held in idolatrous veneration, this appropriation of his ſpoils to the enrichment of his conquerors, are events which will probably lead the way to the complete fall and deſtruction of the capital of this Antichriſtian power, when the meaſure of its abominations ſhall be filled up. Lowman obſerves[a], and it is an important obſervation, that " the fifth vial or cup is poured out on the *throne* of the beaſt; ſo the word is in the original. In the Scripture language,

[a] Lowman, p. 265.

throne,

throne, kingdom, government, authority, dominion and power, are of like signification."......"The throne then of the beast, which our translation has rendered *seat*, seems plainly to mean his authority and power, rather than the city or seat of his residence. For the Prophetic language puts a throne to signify, not the seat of a kingdom, but its power and authority. And so this very Prophecy explains it: this angel poured his vial on the *seat of the beast, and his kingdom was full of darkness*. Darkness is an emblem of affliction; a kingdom full of darkness, will then naturally signify a great diminution of power, and decay of authority: so that the distinguishing punishment of the beast in *this* period, that his kingdom shall be full of darkness, will most properly mean some great and successful opposition to the Papal power and authority, which shall much weaken and lessen it, and give such uneasiness to the supporters of it,

as

as shall drive them into a rage, and make them bite their tongues as it were, for anger and vexation."

The final destruction of Rome is likewise clearly set forth, particularly by St. John in the Prophecies which have been quoted [b], together with the *reasons* on account of which this signal and heavy judgment will be inflicted, and the emotions it is calculated to raise in the minds of mankind.

" The last act which the secular powers [c] shall perform towards this whore, or capital city, is, that they shall destroy her with fire and sword; and by that means leave no refuge there to any of her lovers to hold up, and maintain by her power, the idolatry and tyrannical dominion exercised by her. Most cer-

[b] Introductory Chapter, p. 11.
[c] Daubuz, p. 798.

tainly thefe fymbols imply the entire deftruction of this capital city......Thus her fate will be like that of the literal Babylon, whofe fituation is now almoft unknown, becaufe it has been utterly deftroyed. The fall of this myftical Babylon muft make way to the fall of idolatry; it feems morally impoffible that the one fhould be done without the other. And when we confider the conftant method of the divine Providence, which has been to include the capital in the fate of the nation condemned, as Nineveh, Babylon, Jerufalem, Samaria, and fome others; why fhould we think it will be more favourable to Rome, the city which has been a greater and more conftant enemy to the true religion, both in the Jewifh and the Chriftian difpenfations, than any other; and has tyrannized with the moft horrid aggravations beyond any thing before? This Chapter puts it out of doubt, that the utter deftruction of Rome is defigned

by

by the Almighty. Neverthelefs as it will appear afterwards by the nineteenth Chapter, fome confiderable part of the favourers of idolatry and tyranny fhall ftill fubfift after the *fall* of this Babylon, and keep up the old pretenfions of the beaft, and falfe Prophet, till they are deftroyed by a judgment there defcribed and foretold. But in the mean time they fhall never be able to reftore Babylon to its former ftate."

" [d] It appears then that this Antichriftian power was to arife in the latter times of the Roman Empire, after an end fhould be put to the imperial power, and after the empire fhould be divided into ten kingdoms: and it is not only foretold *when* it fhould prevail, but moreover *how long* it fhould prevail. Here we cannot but obferve, that the very fame period of time is prefixed for

[d] Newton, vol. iii. p. 395, 396.

its continuance both by Daniel and by St. John. Wonderful is the confent and harmony between thefe infpired writers, as in other circumftances of the Prophecy, fo particularly in this. In Daniel *the little horn* was to *wear out the faints of the moft High, and think to change times and laws*; and it is faid exprefsly, that they *fhould be given into his hand, until a time, and times, and the dividing of time*; or as the fame thing is expreffed in another place, *for a time, times, and a half.* In the Revelation it is faid of *the beaft,* to whom in like manner *it was given to make war with the faints, and to overcome them,* that *power* alfo *was given unto him to continue forty and two months:* and *the holy city the Gentiles fhould tread under foot forty and two months:* and *the two witneffes fhould prophefy a thoufand two hundred and threefcore days clothed in fackcloth:* and the woman, the true church of Chrift, who fled into the wildernefs from perfecution, fhould be fed and

and nourished there *a thousand two hundred and threescore days*, or as it is otherwise expressed in the same chapter, *for a time, and times, and half a time.* Now all these numbers you will find upon computation to be the same, and each of them to signify 1260 years. For *a time is a year*, and *a time and times and the dividing of time*, or *half a time*, are three years and a half, and *three years and a half*, are 42 *months*, and 42 *months* are 1260 *days*, and 1260 *days* in the Prophetic style are 1260 *years.* From all these dates and characters it may fairly be concluded, that the time of the church's great affliction and of the reign of Antichrist will be a period of 1260 years."

The conjectures concerning the *exact* date of the commencement of this Antichristian power are so numerous, that it will be prudent to wait for its end before we form a decided opinion. We have however fufficient ground to conclude pofitively, that from whatever remarkable era thefe prophetical years are dated, the period of their accomplifhment cannot be *very* remote from the prefent times—Fleming " reckons that the Papal head took its *rife* from that memorable year 606, when Phocas did in a manner devolve the government of the *Weft* upon Boniface III. by giving him the title of *fupreme* and univerfal Bifhop; or in 608, when Boniface IV. did firft publicly authorize idolatry, by dedicating the Pantheon to the worfhip of the Virgin Mary, and all faints; but he does not confider his power as eftablifhed, till fome years afterwards.—By *fteps* he hath been *raifed up*, and by *fteps* muft he be *pulled down*."—" In the year 666, the myftical number of the beaft, which Irenæus interpreted to mean the Latin Monarchy, Pope Vitalian did firft ordain that *all public worfhip* fhould be in *Latin*"—In 756, or 758, which was 666 years after St. John faw the vifion of the beaft, according to the moft probable calculation, Pope Paul I. received the exarchate of Ravenna as a donation from *Pepin, King of France*, and then was his power *fully eftablifhed.*—Bifhop Newton confiders the year 727 as the moft probable era, for the *rife* of this power, as the Pope and people of Rome in that year revolted from the Exarch of Ravenna, and fhook off their allegiance to the Greek Emperor; and Sigonius obferves, that in 727 " Rome and the Roman *dukedom* came from the Greeks to the Roman Pontiff"—The Pope *then* became a *little* horn, or fecular prince; but his power was not *fully eftablifhed*, till he obtained the exarchate of Ravenna from Pepin, in 756, or 758. It is very remarkable, that whether we adopt Fleming's mode of calculation, and date the beginning of the 1260 years from 758, when *all* agree that the Papacy was *fully* eftablifhed as a *temporal*, as well as spiritual power; or whether, with Bishop Newton [d], and according to common calculation, we consider " the beginning of the 1260 years of the reign of Antichrist, is to be dated from the year 727, their end will fall near the year 2000 after Christ; and at the end of the 6000th year of the world, when, according to a very early tradition of Jews and Christians, and even of Heathens, great changes and revolutions are expected both in the natural and in the moral world; and *there remaineth*, according to the words of the Apostle, a *sabbatism, or holy rest to the people of God*."

Thus was the Antichristian power of the Church of Rome described by Daniel, St. Paul, and St. John, at a time when no such power existed, as it was to be in future and distant ages, in the rise, progress, and establishment of its

[d] Newton, vol. iii. p. 397.

temporal and spiritual dominion. They pointed out, in a manner strictly correspondent with the whole series of the history of that Church, its departure from the true faith, its errors, ceremonies, pretended miracles and canonizations of martyrs, the greatness of its authority, and the boundless extent of its dominion: they even marked with more appropriate circumstances, its spirit of intolerance and persecution, its monastic establishments, the celibacy of its clergy, its impious assumption of a divine power to grant pardons and absolutions for sin; the departure of the Protestants from its communion, its gradual decline, and its final destruction.

" ᵉ If in the days of St. Paul and St. John, there were any footsteps of such a sort of *Power* as this in the world; or if there ever *had been* any such power in

ᵉ Clarke's Evidences of Natural and Revealed Religion, vol. ii. p. 720.

the world; or if there was then any appearance or probability, that there ever *could be* any such kind of power in the world; much less in the TEMPLE or Church of God; and if there be not now [or very lately was] such a Power *actually* and *conspicuously* exercised in the Christian world; and if any picture of this Power, drawn *after the* EVENT, can *now* describe it more plainly and exactly, than it was *originally* described in the words of THESE PROPHECIES; THEN, BUT NOT TILL THEN, may it with some degree of plausibleness be suggested by an Atheist or a Deist, that these Prophecies are nothing more than enthusiastic imaginations."

CLASS II.

CHAPTER THE SECOND.

THE RISE, PROGRESS, ESTABLISHMENT, AND DECLINE OF THE MAHOMETAN POWER OF ANTICHRIST.

WE have already seen[a] that the Prophets Daniel and St. John clearly revealed the rise and establishment of a Power in *the East*, at *a certain period of time*, which was to be a scourge " to the people of God" for their manifold offences; and which is to be considered as one of the forms of Antichrist.—We now proceed to prove, from the authority of the most eminent and learned Commentators, Mede, Vitringa, Dau-

[a] See Introductory Chapter, p. 13.

buz,

buz, Sir Ifaac and Bifhop Newton, More, Whifton, Lowman, and many others, and from the teftimony of *Hiftorical facts*, that thefe Prophecies are ftrictly applicable to Mahomet and his followers—that they have been accomplifhed, by them as far as time will admit of their accomplifhment, and are at the prefent hour fulfilling before our eyes.

In the ninth chapter of Revelations, which the Reader will recollect was quoted at length in page 13. St. John has prefigured under fuitable emblems, the origin, the characteriftic manners, the arts of war, and the deftructive ravages of the pretended Prophet of Arabia and his followers—the Arabians, Saracens, and Turks—upon the idolatrous and corrupt Chriftians. This formidable power. commenced about the year of Chrift 606, which is confidered by moft of the *early* Commentators, as the

the year when the Papal Antichrift was *firft* eftablifhed[a].

By the permiffion of Divine providence, whofe defigns are frequently reprefented in Scripture, and more particularly in the Apocalypfe, as being accomplifhed by celeftial agents; an angel defcended and opened *the cave of the abyfs*, for fo the words of the original Greek ought to be tranflated. This figurative reprefentation properly expreffes a commiffion from heaven to allow Satan to infeft the world with fome new and great trial. "[b] The word ftand-

---

[a] It is fomewhat remarkable that thefe powers not only arofe, but were *fully eftablifhed* nearly together. In the year 758 the Pope received the exarchate of Ravenna, and foon after became fovereign of Rome. In 762, the Saracen Caliph, Almanfor, built Bagdad as the *capital* of his extenfive empire. It is certain that they have *declined* together, and the popular opinion in Rome and Conftantinople concerning their fall is fingularly fimilar.

[b] Whitaker's View of the Proph. p. 119, 20, 21.

ing

ing in the original for *cave*, is more particularly expreffive of thofe caverns, which, on account of the fprings they contain, emit a vapour, and were by Pagan fuperftition often confidered as the feats of oracles and fources of infpiration. And does not this emblem moſt ſtrikingly defcribe the rife of a pretended revelation? Or, when fuch, anfwering in all points to the prediction, was propagated at the period to which this Prophecy relates, does not the *literal* circumſtance of its rife from a cave, both fix the application, and demonſtrate the truth of the Prophecy? And that fuch was the origin of the Koran of Mahomet, we learn from Mr. Gibbon's declaration, that Mahomet during the month Ramadan in each year, withdrew from the world to the cave of Hera, 'and confulted the fpirit of fraud and enthufiafm." *The fun and the air were darkened by reafon of the fmoke of the pit*, when the falfehoods, contradictions, and

and fables of the Koran ufurped the place of the Gofpel truths. And that the preaching of Mahomet brought on a fpiritual darknefs, by obfcuring the light of Revelation, the fate of the Gofpel in the countries ruled by his difciples fufficiently proves, without taking into the account the following words of the hiftorian, when defcribing the treatment of Chriftians dwelling in Mahometan countries.—"^c A *decent reverence* for the national faith is impofed on their fermons and converfations: and the facrilegious attempt to feduce a Muffulman will not be fuffered to efcape with impunity.—In a time however of tranquillity and juftice, the Chriftians have never been compelled to renounce the Gofpel or to embrace the Koran; but the punifhment of death is inflicted for the apoftates, who have profeffed and deferted the law of Mahomet."—Reftric-

[c] Gibbon, c. 51.

tions,

tions like thefe, and efpecially the *laſt*, when laid upon the leſſons of truth, amount to obſcuring it; though we add not the effect of other circumſtances which have impeded the influence of the Goſpel, and diminiſhed the number of its difciples in the regions under the dominion of the Muſſulmen."

As out of the ſmoke came locuſts upon the earth, ſo the pretended divine miſſion of Mahomet was the immediate cauſe of the Saracens overrunning the countries they infeſted; and the Hiſtorian before quoted gives us ſufficient proofs of the connexion between the doctrines they taught, and the conqueſts they atchieved; and of the facility of eſtabliſhing ſuch a connexion in minds ſo ardent, and tempers ſo enthuſiaſtic as thoſe of his followers. "[d] The Prophet of Medina aſſumed in his *new* Revelations a fiercer and more ſanguinary tone, which proves

[d] Gibbon, c. 50.

that

that his former moderation was the effect of weakness: the means of persuasion had been tried, the season of forbearance was elapsed; and he was now commanded to propagate his religion by the sword, to destroy the monuments of idolatry, and, without regarding the sanctity of days or months, to pursue the unbelieving nations of the earth."..... " From all sides the roving Arabs were allured to the standard of religion and plunder."...." Their intrepid souls were fired with enthusiasm, the enjoyment of wealth and beauty was held out as the reward of their victory over Christians and idolaters, the picture of the invisible world was strongly painted on their imagination; and the death which they had always despised, became an object of hope and desire."

The King who led these vast armies is not only mentioned, but emphatically described as *the angel of the bottomless pit, or abyss,*

abyss, whose name in the Hebrew tongue is A-baddon, but in the Greek tongue hath his name Apollyon. The title *Abaddon,* is remarked by the learned Joseph Mede to be an allusion to Obodas, the common name of the antient monarchs of that part of Arabia, from whence Mahomet came. Such in prophetical language was He who issued from the *abyss,* or *cave of Hera,* to propagate his pretended revelations; such was He who pretended that he received his instructions by the ministration of the *angel* Gabriel, and who alleged a divine commission to justify bloodshed and destruction. Mahomet professedly declared, that his faith was not to be extended by miracles, or by any gentle means, but by force of arms. " [e] The sword," said he, " is the key of heaven and of hell : a drop of blood shed in the cause of God, a night spent in arms, is of more avail, than two months of

[e] Gibbon, c. 50.

fasting

fasting or prayer: whoever falls in battle, his sins are forgiven; at the day of judgment his wounds shall be resplendent as vermilion, and as odoriferous as musk: and the loss of his limbs shall be supplied by the wings of angels and of cherubim." The whole course of his conduct was consistent with these declarations, and his bloody career was marked by the sacrifice of the laws of justice and the feelings of humanity, to his revenge and his ambition. "He fought in person at nine battles, or sieges; and fifty enterprises of war were atchieved in ten years by himself or his lieutenants.....The use of fraud and perfidy, of cruelty and injustice, were often subservient to the propagation of the faith; and Mahomet commanded, or approved the assassination of the Jews and idolaters who had escaped from the field of battle."

Under the banners of this DESTROY-ER, and "his succeffors, went forth the armies of Arabs and Saracens *like locufts upon the earth* for their numbers and the rapidity of their progrefs; and *like fcorpions of the earth* for their venom, and their power to inflict the moft deadly wounds. Gibbon calls them, "*Flights of Barbarians*;" and the Arabian writers defcribe the followers of Mahomet *as fwarms of locufts* flying into a country to confume its productions. And yet they are commanded, *that they fhould not hurt the grafs of the earth, neither any green thing, neither any tree.* The locufts of the Prophecy are therefore not real, but typical locufts, and an hiftorical fact will fhow how well this reftriction applies to the Mahometan armies. The Caliph A-bubeker[f], who fucceeded Mahomet in the year 632, gave exprefs orders to Ye-

[f] Lowman, p. 123.

fid the General of his forces, not to deſtroy any palm-trees, nor burn any fields of corn, nor cut down any fruit-trees.

The fury and deſtructive ravages of the Arabs and Saracens were directed againſt the degenerate Chriſtians, and they were raiſed up as the terrible inſtruments of the divine difpleaſure, *to hurt thoſe men who had not the ſeal of God in their foreheads.* Here is a deſcription, concife indeed, but fufficiently characteriſtic of the Chriſtians at the commencement of the ſeventh century, when Mahomet began to propagate his faith. *They had not the ſeal of God in their foreheads*—they were not diſtinguiſhed by the proper marks of their Chriſtian profeſſion. Such was the fact as we collect it from all the hiſtorians of thoſe times, and more particularly from Gibbon, who in his fortieth, forty-firſt, forty-third, and forty-fifth Chapters, has drawn, with a malignant pleaſure, the dark picture of of their enmities, their corruptions, and their vices. Of their superstition and idolatrous tendency, which appear evidently from the concluding part of the Prophecy, to be particular objects of the divine punishment, he thus speaks— " The Christians of the seventh century had insensibly relapsed into a semblance of Paganism: their public and private vows were addressed to the relics and images that disgraced the temples of the East: the throne of the Almighty was darkened by a cloud of martyrs, and saints, and angels, the objects of popular veneration; and the Collyridian Heretics, who flourished in the fruitful soil of Arabia, invested the Virgin Mary with the name and honours of a goddess." ^g The parts of the world which remained most free from these corruptions, were Savoy, Piedmont, and the southern parts of France (which were

---

^g Newton, vol. iii. p. 101.

after-

afterwards the nurseries and habitations of the Albigenses and Waldenses), and on this account they escaped the calamities of the times. For it ought to be particularly noticed, that when the Saracens approached these countries in the year 732, they were defeated with great slaughter in several engagements, by the renowned Charles Martel, King of France[h].

To them it was given that they should not kill them, but that they should be tormented. In the course of the succesful inroads made by the Saracens, no government, state, or empire, was *killed, or destroyed.* "[i] They greatly harrassed and tormented both the Greek and the Latin Churches; but they did not utterly extirpate the one or the other. They besieged Constantinople, and even plun-

[h] Gibbon, c. 53.
[i] Newton, vol. iii. p. 101.

dered Rome; but they could not make themselves masters of either of those capital cities. The Greek Empire suffered most from them, as it was nearest to their own territories. They dismembered it of Syria, and of Egypt, and some others of its best and richest provinces; but they were never able to subdue and conquer the whole. As often as they besieged Constantinople, they were repulsed and defeated. They attempted it in the reign of Constantine Pogonatus, A. D. 672; but their men and ships were destroyed by the sea-fire invented by Callinicus; and, after seven years ineffectual pains, they were compelled to raise the siege and conclude a peace. They attempted it again in the reign of Leo Isauricus, A. D. 718; but they were forced to desist by famine, and pestilence, and losses of various kinds. In this attempt they exceeded their commission; and therefore they were not crowned with their usual success." Although

though the followers of Mahomet did not fubvert the governments of the countries which they invaded, yet their military laws adjudged fo many people to captivity, and the condition of the women in particular was fo deplorable [k], being fo much in the power of perfons who fet no bounds to their paffions, that *in thofe days men fought death, and could not find it, and they defired to die, and death was far from them.* They preferred death to the hard conditions of flavery and oppreffion to which they were reduced, and earneftly wifhed to clofe the fcene of their miferies and their lives together.

The vaft armies which followed the ftandard of Mahomet were compofed of cavalry—*they were like unto horfes prepared for battle.*—The Arabs were always celebrated for the excellent breed of

---

[k] Lowman, p. 123.

their horfes, their expertnefs in all equef-
trian exercifes, and the great advantages
they derived from their fwift and well
appointed cavalry in their various wars
and incurfions. *On their heads were as it
were crowns like gold*—The turban was
the peculiar drefs of the Arabian chiefs,
adorned with plates or bands of gold.
And as the crown is an emblem of fovereignty, the prophetical allufion may
refer to the numerous kingdoms which
they overran. For as Mr. Mede excel-
lently obferves[1], " No nation had ever
fo wide a command, nor ever were fo
many kingdoms, fo many regions fubju-
gated in fo fhort a fpace of time. It
founds incredible, yet moft true it is,
that in the fpace of eighty or not many
more years, they fubdued and acquired
to the diabolical kingdom of Mohammed, Paleftine, Syria, both Armenias,
almoft all Afia Minor, Perfia, India, E-

---

[1] Newton, vol. iii. p. 103.

gypt, Numidia, all Barbary, even to the river Niger, Portugal and Spain. Neither did their fortune or ambition ſtop here, till they had added alſo a great part of Italy, as far as to the gates of Rome; moreover Sicily, Candia, Cyprus, and the other iſlands of the Mediterranean Sea. Good God! how great a tract of land! how many *crowns* were here! Whence alſo it is worthy of obſervation, that mention is not made here, as in other trumpets, *of the third part*; foraſmuch as this plague fell no leſs without the bounds of the Roman Empire than within it, and extended itſelf even to the remoteſt Indies."

*Their faces were as the faces of men—*they had a bold and manly countenance—but they wore their hair in an effeminate manner. *They had their hair as the hair of women.*—The Saracens let their hair grow to a great length, and wore it plaited, and in treſſes. [m] It was obſerved by Pliny, that the Arabians wore a kind of turbans, or mitres on their heads; that they dreſſed and twiſted their hair in a particular manner; ſo that one part of the Saracens was diſtinguiſhed by it from another. *Their teeth were as the teeth of lions*—They were as well furniſhed with the inſtruments of deſtruction, as if nature had given them the teeth of the ſtrongeſt animals.—*And they had breaſt-plates, as it were of iron*—Well furniſhed with the means of deſtruction, they were equally well equipped with defenſive armour. As the locuſt is defended by a hard ſhell of the colour of iron, ſo the Saracens were guarded by coats of mail calculated to repel the darts and other weapons of their enemies[n]. Their formidable and cla-

[m] Lowman, p. 121.

[n] *" The ſound of their wings denotes the ſwiftneſs*

clamorous onset, when hastening forward to engage their enemies, was as *the sound of chariots of many horses running to battle.*

The exact season of the year, during which the Saracens made their most remarkable ravages and conquests, is repeatedly pointed out. The men whom they assailed, *were tormented five months*[o]. The locusts infest the countries of the East for the five warmest months, and they are inactive and torpid for the rest of the year. It is well known, that the manner in which the Arabs invaded their neighbours, was by sudden incursions during the summer months; retiring again and dispersing during the winter, and gathering together the next spring,

---

ness and rapidity of their conquests; and it is indeed astonishing, that in less than a century they erected an empire, which extended from India to Spain. Newton.

[o] Lowman, p. 122.

for a new fummer's invafion. According to the military laws and conftitutions of the Mahometans, war was forbid during the facred months, which were the two firft and the two laft. The prophetical defcription is not lefs exact in a figurative, than in a literal fenfe. The days that conftitute the months, in which *men were tormented*, may be reckoned as equivalent to 150 years, according to the ufual mode of prophetical computation[p]. Within the fpace of thefe 150 years, the Saracens made their greateft conquefts[q]. Mahomet emerged from the

[p] Newton, vol. iii. p. 109.

[q] The number being repeated twice, the fums may be thought to be doubled, and amount in prophetic computation to 300 years: then, according to Sir I. Newton, "The whole time that the Caliphs of the Saracens reigned with a temporal dominion at Damafcus and Bagdad together, was 300 years, viz. from the year 637 to the year 936, inclufive;" when their empire was broken and divided into feveral principalities, or kingdoms.

So

the *cave of the abyss*, and began to propagate his religion in the year 612; and Bagdat, or the city of peace, was built by the Caliph Almanfor, in the year 762." This was the firſt fixed eſtabliſhment of the Caliphs, where they enjoyed the fruits of their conqueſts, and funk in luxury and repoſe. "ʳ In this city of peace, amidſt the riches of the Eaſt, the Abaſſides foon difdained the abſtinence and frugality of the firſt Caliphs, and aſpired to emulate the magnificence of the Perſian kings. After his wars and buildings, Almanfor left behind him in gold and filver about thirty millions ſterling, and this treaſure was exhauſted in a few years, by the vices or virtues of his children." After the period deſtined for the ravages of the *locuſts*, the rage of

---

So that let theſe *five months* be taken in any poſſible conſtruction, the event will ſtill anſwer, and the Prophecy will ſtill be fulfilled." Newton, vol. iii. p. 110, 111.

ʳ Gibbon, c. 52.

the Saracens for conqueft and plunder began to fubfide, the *torments* inflicted by thefe fatal *fcorpions* began to abate, and the diftrefs and defolation, which they had fpread over fo confiderable a portion of the earth, received an extraordinary check from their own inteftine difputes, and the fettlement of eftablifhed monarchies in Perfia, Africa, and Spain. "*The fovereignty of Arabia was loft by the extent and the rapidity of conqueft. The colonies of the nation were fcattered over the Eaft and the Weft, and their blood was mingled with the blood of their converts and captives. After the reign of three Caliphs, the throne was tranfported from Medina to the valley of Damafcus, and the banks of the Tigris; the holy cities were violated by impious war; Arabia was ruled by the rod of a fubject, perhaps of a ftranger; and the Bedoweens of the de-

* Gibbon, c. 50.

fert,

fert, awakening from their dream of dominion, refumed their old and folitary independence."

Notwithftanding fuch great and fignal punifhments were inflicted upon the Chriftians of the *Eaſt*, and of the *South*, and of the *Weſt*, by the propagation of the falfe religion of Mahomet, and by the oppreffions exercifed over them by the Saracen locufts, yet no general reformation was produced either in the eftablifhment or the manners of the Chriftians. In vain did the Emperor Leo the Ifaurian, and his fon Conftantinus Copronymus in the year 718, endeavour to put a ftop to the idolatrous practice of image-worfhip; and in order to abolifh it effectually, ordered all images to be taken from the churches. *Their exertions were violently oppofed by the Bifhops of Rome.* Gregory II. confirmed the prevailing idolatry by the authority of a Synod, rejected the order
of

of the Emperor, abfolved his fubjects from their allegiance, and even proceeded to excommunicate him, and he obtained a confirmation of the prevailing fuperftitions both in the Eaft and in the Weft, by the decrees of general councils. Of this incorrigible wickednefs we find notice given by the prediction of the woes which were to follow.

One woe is paft, behold there come two woes more hereafter. This mode of expreffion evidently fhows that between the ceafing of the firft woe, and the beginning of the fecond there fhould be fome interval of time. [t] With this intimation the event exactly correfponded, fince the power prefigured by the four angels bound in the Euphrates [u] did not invade

[t] Whitaker, p. 135.
[u] The great river Euphrates, to whofe banks they had been confined, defcends from the mountains of Armenia, runs through the provinces of Chaldea

invade the territories of the Roman Empire, nor torment the Chriſtians, who were eſtabliſhed in it, till ſome centuries had elapſed after the ceſſation of the ravages of the Saracens.

One of the tribes of the Turks indeed made an irruption into the Greek Empire, ſooner than the time allotted for the advance of "the Euphratean horſemen." "ˣ Twenty-five years after the death of Baſil, his ſucceſſors, in the year 1050, were ſuddenly aſſaulted by an unknown race of Barbarians, who united the Scythian valour with the fanaticiſm of new proſelytes, and the arts and riches of a powerful monarchy. The *myriads* of Turkiſh horſemen overſpread a frontier of ſix hundred miles, from Tauris to Arzeroum : and *the blood of one hundred*

Chaldea and Babylon, and is the centre of the Turkiſh dominions.
ˣ Gibbon, c. 57.

and

and thirty thousand Christians was a grateful sacrifice to the Arabian Prophet." But the Prophets notice only that particular nation, whose firmly established empire has lasted to the present day.

In the year 1055, Togrul Beg, Sultan of the Turks, after having subdued Chorazin and Persia, took possession of Bagdad, the capital of the Saracen Caliphs. His successors, Olub Anslam, and Melech Schah, conquered the regions of the Euphrates; and after the death of Melech Schah, these conquests were broken into the kingdoms of Armenia, Mesopotamia, Syria, and Cappadocia, the capitals of which were Mizapharekin, Mosul, Aleppo, and Iconium, according to Sir I. Newton. Bishop Newton supposes these sultanies to take their names from the cities of Bagdad, Damascus, Aleppo, and Iconium, at the periods they settled themselves there; but this difference does not affect the point

point in queftion. Thefe four Sultans were for a confiderable time " bound," or reftrained from extending their conquefts farther than the territories bordering on the Euphrates, by the croifades of the European Chriftians into the Holy Land, in the latter part of the eleventh, and in the twelfth and thirteenth centuries. Religion probably forbad their molefting the Saracens during the attack of their Chriftian enemies. But when the Chriftians abandoned their conquefts in Syria and Paleftine, then " the four angels in the river Euphrates were loofed." Soliman Shah [y], the firft chief and founder of the Othman race, was drowned in his attempt to pafs the Euphrates, in his retreat from Jengis Chan: but Ortogrul, his third fon, obtained leave of Aladin, Sultan of Iconium, to fettle in the mountains of Armenia, with 400 of his Turks. " From

[y] Newton, vol. iii. p. 114.

thence they began their excursions; and the other Turks associating with them, and following their standard, they gained several victories over the Tartars on one side, and over the Christians on the other. Ortogrul dying in 1288, Othman, or Osman, his son succeeded him in power and authority; and in 1299, as some say, with the consent of Aladin himself, he was proclaimed Sultan, and founded a new empire; and the people afterwards [a mixed multitude, the remains of the four Sultanies] as well as the new empire, was called by his name."

"[z] In this manner, and at this particular time, *the four angels were loosed to slay the third part of men*, that is, to conquer and to overthrow the subjects of the Roman Empire. The Latin or Western Empire was broken to pieces under the first four trumpets; the

---

[z] Newton, vol. iii. p. 116.

Greek or Eastern empire was cruelly *hurt*, and *tormented* under the fifth trumpet; and here under the sixth trumpet it is to be *slain* and utterly destroyed. Accordingly all Asia Minor, Syria, Palestine, Egypt, Thrace, Macedon, Greece, and all the countries which formerly belonged to the Greek or Eastern Emperors, the Othmans have conquered and subjugated to their dominion. They first passed over into Europe, in the reign of Orchan their second emperor, in the year 1357. They took Constantinople in the reign of Mohammed their seventh emperor, in the year 1453; and in time all the remaining parts of the Greek Empire shared the fate of their capital city. * The last of their conquests were Candia, or the antient Crete, in 1669, and Cameniec in 1672. For the execution of this great work, it is said that they *were prepared for an hour,*

* Newton, vol. iii. p. 117.

and a day, and a month, and a year. Now it is wonderfully remarkable, that the firſt conqueſt mentioned in hiſtory, of the Othmans over the Chriſtians, was in the year of the Hegira 680, and the year of Chriſt 1281. For Ortogrul ' in that year (according to the accurate Hiſtorian Saadi) crowned his victories with the conqueſt of the famous city of Kutahi upon the Greeks.' Compute 391 years from that time [according to eſtabliſhed prophetic calculation] and they will terminate in the year 1672 : and in that year, as it was hinted before, Mohammed the fourth took Cameniec from the Poles; ' and forty-eight towns and villages in the territory of Cameniec were delivered up' to the Sultan upon the treaty of peace. Whereupon Prince Cantemir hath made this memorable reflexion, ' This was the laſt victory by which any advantage accrued to the Othman ſtate; or any city or province was annexed to the ancient bounds of the

the empire.' Agreeably to which obfervation, he hath intitled the former part of his hiftory, *Of the growth of the Othman Empire*, and the following part, *Of the decay of the Othman Empire*. Other wars and flaughters, as he fays, have enfued. The Turks even befieged Vienna in 1683; but this exceeding the bounds of their commiffion, they were defeated. Belgrade and other places may have been taken from them, and furrendered to them again: but ftill they have fubdued no new ftate or potentate of Chriftendom now for the fpace of between 80 and 90 years; and in all probability they never may again, their empire appearing rather to decreafe than increafe. Here then the Prophecy and the event agree exactly in the period of 391 years; and if more accurate and authentic hiftories of the Othmans were brought to light, and we knew the very day wherein Kutahi was taken, as certainly as we know that wherein Cameniec was taken,

the

the like exactnefs might alfo be found in the 15 days. But though the time be limited for the Othmans *flaying the third part of men*, yet no time is fixed for the duration of their empire; only this fecond woe will end, when the third woe, or the deftruction of the beaft, fhall be at hand [b]."

And the number of the army of the horfemen were two hundred thoufand thoufand, or as the words may be tranflated more literally, " two myriads of myriads." It was the cuftom of the Tartarian tribes to count their forces by myriads; and Gibbon, fpeaking of the Turkifh cavalry, adopts this mode of computation. The Hiftorian, defcribing the peculiar manners and cuftoms of their anceftors, says [c], their wandering life maintains the fpirit and exercife of

---

[b] See the fecond Introductory Chapter.
[c] Gibbon, c. 57.

arms;

arms; *they fight on horseback*.....[d] The Sultan Mahmud inquired of a chief of the race of Seljuk, who dwelt in the territory of Bochara, what supply of men he could furnish for military service. If you send, replied Ismael, one of these arrows into our camp, *fifty thousand* of your servants *will mount on horseback*. And if that number, continued Mahmud, should not be sufficient? Send this second arrow to the horde of Balik, and you will find *fifty thousand* more. But, said the Sultan, if I should stand in need of your whole kindred tribes? Dispatch my bow, was the last reply of Ismael, and as it is circulated around, the summons will be obeyed by *two hundred thousand horse*.

A. D. 1038.

[e] When Alp Arslan invaded the Roman Empire, " his hopes of victory were

A. D. 1071.

[d] Gibbon, c. 57. p. 650.
[e] Gibbon, c. 57.

placed

placed in the arrows of the *Turkish cavalry*, whose squadrons were loosely distributed in the form of a crescent." [f] At the last siege of Constantinople in the numerous army of Turks, which consisted of *two hundred and fifty-eight thousand* men, there were, according to an historian quoted by Gibbon, only fifteen thousand Janizaries, troops which are known to be the principal infantry of the Ottomans;—so that if an allowance be made for forty thousand foot, collected together under other denominations, there will remain for the number of the army of the horsemen on this single occasion, literally *twenty myriads*, or two hundred thousand [g]."

Those

[f] Whitaker, p. 151.

[g] "The Timariots, or Horsemen holding lands by serving in the wars, are the strength of the Turkish government; and these, as Heylin affirms, are in all accounted between seven and eight hundred thousand fighting men: some say that they

are

Those that sat upon the horses had breastplates of fire, and of jacinct, and brimstone. ʰ The colour of fire is red, of hyacinth, or jacinct, blue, and of brimstone yellow: and this, as Daubuz observes, hath a literal accomplishment; for the Othmans, from the first time of their appearance, have affected to wear such warlike apparel of scarlet, blue, and yellow. Of the Spahis particularly, some have red, and some have yellow standards, and others red or yellow, mixed with other colours. In appearance too *the heads of their horses were as the heads of lions*, to denote their strength, courage, and fierceness.

The fire, smoke, and brimstone, which are represented as *issuing out of the mouths of the horses*, immediately suggest the

---

are a million; and besides these, there are Spahis and other horsemen in the Emperor's pay." Newton, vol. iii. p. 121.

ʰ Newton, vol. iii. p. 121.

idea of gunpowder, which was not invented till this trumpet founded another woe to "the third part of men." The Turks not only used fire-arms in their military expeditions, but such cannon as were of a most enormous size. To this fact the historian bears ample testimony in the following passages. "[1] Among the implements of destruction Mahomet II. studied with peculiar care, the recent and tremendous discovery of the Latins: [in the fifteenth century] *and his artillery surpassed whatever had yet appeared in the world.*—A foundery was established at Adrianople; the metal was prepared; and at the end of three months, Urban (the cannon-founder) produced a piece of brass ordnance of stupendous and almost incredible magnitude. A measure of twelve palms is assigned to the bore; and the stone bullet weighed above six hundred pounds.".…

[1] Gibbon, c. 68.

And

And again in the same chapter, "The great cannon of Mahomet has been separately noticed, *an important and visible object in the history of the times:* but that enormous engine was flanked by two fellows almost of equal magnitude: the long order of Turkish artillery was pointed against the walls; fourteen batteries thundered at once on the most accessible places; and at one of these it is ambiguously expressed, that it was mounted with one hundred and thirty guns, or that it discharged one hundred and thirty bullets." With such engines was Constantinople, the capital of the world, overthrown: and thus was realized the symbol of *one third of men being killed by the fire, smoke, and brimstone proceeding out of their mouths*. Mahomet II. took the isthmus of Peloponnesus, and spread a general consternation throughout Greece. Two hundred and sixty towns in Christendom yielded to the power of his arms; and for his great success in war, he was principally indebted to the myriads, that compofed his cavalry, and the number and enormous fize of his cannon[k].

[l] The laft particular noticed by St. John in his defcription of the Ottomans, is, that, like the locufts, *with their tails they do hurt. For their power is in their mouths, and in their tails: for their tails were like unto ferpents, and had heads, and with them they do hurt.* That under the Turkifh empire, the falfe doctrine of Mahomet has been fpread with no lefs zeal than under the Saracens, is too well known to need the teftimony of hiftory:

[k] There is in the arfenal of Conftantinople the breech of a cannon which was melted in a fire a century ago, of a moft enormous fize (I am forry I have not the meafure of it); but thofe of the Dardanelles are diminutive in comparifon to it. It was one of thofe ufed at the fiege of Conftantinople. *Eton's Survey of the Turkifh Empire*, p. 95.
[l] Whitaker, p. 153.

yet,

yet, to show that our Historian continues to bear witness to this Prophecy, we transcribe a passage, which may be considered as containing a reason for the power of their mouths, and their tails to hurt being so closely conjoined in the text: since it shows that conquest was the means of propagating the faith. "To propagate the true religion was the duty of a faithful Mussulman: the unbelievers were his (the Sultan Amurath II's) enemies, and those of the Prophet; and in the hands of the Turks, the scymeter was the only instrument of conversion." Wherever they have carried their arms, they have left the poison of their doctrines.

As the Eastern Christians, who had been enlightened by the earliest rays of the Gospel, were the first in the commission of offences, so were they the first that felt the weight of divine punishment. Of this we have memorable examples

amples in the fall of the feven celebrated churches of Afia, to which St. John in the beginning of the Revelation addreffed his admonitions, and his conditional promifes and threats. The infidel Hiftorian, fo often quoted, gives a melancholy picture of their prefent ftate; yet the force of truth draws from his reluctant pen a ftriking conformity between fact and prediction. Is not the *city of Philadelphia in Afia* marked out by the Prophecy as the *peculiar* object of the divine commendation and favour, in. confequence of its fuperior firmnefs and perfeverance in the faith? and has not that city, *even according to the defcription of the Hiftorian himfelf*, been diftinguifhed by the fame *perfeverance*, and remained *independent*, and even *triumphant*, when all the other cities have been either *deftroyed*, or *overpowered* by the Turks?

" [m] And to the angel of the church in

[m] Rev. iii. 7, 8, 9, 10, 11, 12, 13.

Phi-

Philadelphia write, thefe things faith he that is holy, he that is true, he that hath the key of David, he that openeth and no man fhutteth, and fhutteth and no man openeth. *I know thy works; behold I have fet before thee an open door, and no man can fhut it; for thou haft a little ftrength, and haft kept my word, and haft not denied my name. Behold I will make them of the fynagogue of Satan, behold I will make them to come and worfhip before thy feet, and to know that I have loved thee. Becaufe thou haft kept the word of my patience, I alfo will keep thee from the hour of temptation, which fhall come upon all the world, to try them that dwell upon the earth.* Behold, I come quickly: *hold that faft which thou haft, that no man take thy crown. Him that overcometh, will I make a pillar in the temple of my God,* and he fhall go no more out;- and I will write upon him the name of my God, and the name of the city of my God, which is the New

Jerusalem. He that hath an ear, let him hear what the Spirit saith unto the churches."

"ⁿ In the year 1312, the captivity or ruin of the *seven* churches of Asia was consummated; and the barbarous lords of Ionia and Lydia still trample on the monuments of classic and Christian antiquity. In the loss of Ephesus, the Christians deplored the fall of the first angel, the extinction of the first candlestick of the Revelations: the desolation is complete; and the temple of Diana, or the church of Mary, will equally elude the search of the curious traveller. The Circus and three stately theatres of Laodicea are now peopled with wolves and foxes; Sardis is reduced to a miserable village; the God of Mahomet, without a rival or a son, is invoked in the moschs of Thyatira and Pergamus;

ⁿ Gibbon, vol. vi. p. 314.

and

and the populousness of Smyrna is supported by the foreign trade of the Franks and Armenians. *Philadelphia* ALONE *has been saved by Prophecy, or courage.* At a distance from the sea, forgotten by the emperors, *encompassed on all sides by the Turks, her valiant citizens defended their religion and freedom above fourscore years; and at length capitulated with the proudest of the Ottomans.* Among the Greek colonies and churches of Asia, *Philadelphia is still erect; a column in a scene of ruins; a pleasing example, that the paths of honour and safety may sometimes be the same."*

But though the Greek or Eastern Roman Empire, and the Eastern churches, with this single exception, were thus signally overthrown, yet *the rest of men who were not killed by these plagues, repented not of the works of their hands, that they should not worship devils*[o]*, and idols of*

[o] Mahuzzim, δαιμονια, demons, or mediating gods, saints, and angels.

gold and silver, and brass and stone, and wood, which can neither see, nor hear, nor walk; neither repented they of their murders, nor of their sorceries, nor of their fornications, nor of their thefts. The Latin or Western churches, which had suffered but little from *these plagues*, persisted in the worship of saints and images, in their persecutions and inquisitions, pretended miracles, and revelations, in fornication and every species of profligacy, in exactions, impositions, and frauds. But history has recorded their predicted punishment connected with the increase and decline of the Papal power—a subject shortly stated in the preceding Chapter. The Greek or Eastern churches continuing sunk in superstition, idolatry, and wickedness, have, with little exception, been more visibly oppressed by the yoke of Mahometan despotism.

We have seen the exactness with which history has verified the prophetic description

tion of this deftroyer, and traced its rife and progrefs to the meridian of its power. The various and extraordinary marks of decline, fince the period affigned by Prophecy for the height of its elevation, will appear equally ftriking, from a fhort account of the later hiftory, and of the prefent ftate, of the Turkifh Empire, for which the Reader is principally indebted to a recent publication, of great value on account of the illuftrations it fupplies to many parts of this Prophecy[p].

Since the conqueft of Crete and Ca-

[p] The Survey of the Turkifh Empire, by Mr. Eton, many years refident in Turkey, 1798. This work is written with fingular energy, and reflects the higheft credit on its author; not only on account of the ftrong, accurate, and clear views which he gives of the manners and cuftoms of a degenerate and cruel people; but for the application of much political- and commercial knowledge to the arrangement of fuch plans as may promote the interefts of his own country.

menicc

meniec in the year 1672, the sword of *Apollyon*, a term applicable to every Turkish Sultan as well as to Mahomet, has not been *permitted* to subject any other Christian state. The Turks[q] have met with many losses since that memorable period, and have shown evident signs of the decay of their empire, if not of its approaching dissolution. Mustapha II. endeavoured to revive the military ardour of his subjects, by taking the field in person against the Germans; but he was defeated in 1699, by the great Eugene; and the peace of Carlowitz gave to the Emperor the whole province of Transylvania. The inordinate ambition of Achmet III. gained him some advantage over the Russians; but he was reduced, by repeated defeats, to the necessity of concluding a disgraceful peace with the Venetians, and other Christian powers. His war with Kouli

[q] Eton, c. v. p. 129.

Khan,

Khan, the Perfian Ufurper, proved equally unfuccefsful, and terminated in the lofs of his crown, as he was depofed by Mahomet V. in 1730. This prince engaged in a war againft the Ruffians and Germans; but the former advanced againft him with fo much rapidity, as to threaten his capital, and he was therefore compelled to conclude a hafty peace. In the year 1769, Muftapha III. burning with revenge againft the Ruffians, roufed the numerous and favage hordes of Tartars to carry fire and fword into their territories. This was the commencement of a moft bloody war, which was diftinguifhed by the exploits of Prince Gallitzin. He repeatedly attacked the Turkifh armies at Choczim, and gained feveral victories over them; and his career of martial fame was followed by his fucceffor in command, General Romanzoff, who overran Moldavia and Walachia, and received the oaths of allegiance readily offered by their inhabitants,

tants. Soon after a fleet of Ruffians was sent into the Mediterranean, the Turkish Empire was attacked on both sides, and the inhabitants of the Morea, the oppreffed defcendants of the antient Greeks, eager to throw off the yoke of Mahometan defpotifm, flew to arms on the approach of the Ruffians, their Chriftian allies. The naval victory of Tchefmè, a harbour on the coaft of Natolia, added to other fucceffes of the Ruffians, compelled the Porte to conclude a difhonourable peace. This blow was effectually followed up by the fucceeding war, which was terminated in the year 1790, in a manner ftill more favourable to Ruffia[r]. The martial fpirit

of

[r] "It is fcarcely to be doubted that another war, conducted upon fimilar principles, muft totally extinguifh the Turkifh power in Europe—an event defirable to moft Chriftian nations, and particularly to Great Britain. The Ruffian fleet at Sebaftopolis in the Black Sea is now ftrong enough to rifk the

lofs

of the Turks[s], which was formerly animated by religious fanaticifm, has been long in a ftate of decline, and the members, which compofe the vaft body of their empire, are feeble and difunited.

In 1774, with its utmoft efforts,

lofs of half its numbers in an attack on Conftantinople, and the remainder alone might be more than a match for the Sultan's navy." In the laft war the *grand fleet* of the Turks confifted of only feventeen or eighteen fhips of the line, and they have not now near fo many. Eton, p. 81, 193.
   [s] " The inftitution of the Janizaries [by Amurath I.] gave at that time a decifive fuperiority to the Turkifh arms, as they prefented a fyftem of difcipline, and a permanency of organization, till then unknown in Europe. Thefe haughty and celebrated legions were long the terror of furrounding nations, and continued to be looked upon as formidable, until the middle of the feventeenth century. At that time the Turkifh power ceafed to aggrandife itfelf; it *made a paufe in its conquefts, a paufe prophetic of that downfal toward which it has since so rapidly verged*, and which feems now to threaten a fpeedy approach. The fteps which led to this degradation are eafily difcernible." Eton, p. 62.

the

the Turkish empire could only bring 142,000 men into the field[t]; and these numbers, resembling a mob assembled, rather than an army levied, were soon lessened by desertion. In 1773, when the Porte sent 60,000 Janizaries towards Trebizonde, to be embarked for the Crimea, all but 10,000 dispersed themselves on their route[u]. "Their cavalry (which is the only part of their army that deserves the name of regular forces) is as much afraid of their own foot, as of the enemy; for in a defeat they fire at them to get their horses, in order to escape quicker." Their force lies in their attack, but for that they must be prepared; taken unawares, the smallest number puts them to flight: and when their sudden fury of attack is abated, which is at the least obstinate resistance,

[t] Eton, p. 67.
[u] "The hordes of Tartars, which formerly assisted the regular troops, are now principally under the dominion of Russia."

they

they are feized with a panic, and have no rallying as formerly."

"Cafting our view[x] over the pafhaliks, or governments moft immediately connected with the feat of empire, we fhall find them diftracted, diforganized, and fcarcely yielding more than a nominal obedience to the Sultan: fuch are the pafhaliks of Afia Minor and Syria. With regard to the more diftant provinces, they may be confidered connected with the Porte rather by treaty than as integral parts of the empire. In this light I view Moldavia and Walachia in the north, and Egypt in the fouth. Thefe unfortunate countries (unfortunate in their political regulation, however bleffed by the bounty of nature) fuffer, though in different degrees, from the harpy touch of Turkifh defpotifm." The Sultan is the nominal fovereign of Bagd d; but the Pafha has the real power in his

[x] Eton, p. 287.

own

own hands. "[y] In Armenia Major, and all the neighbouring countries, there are whole nations or tribes of independent people, who do not even acknowledge the Porte, or any of its paſhas. The three Arabias do not acknowledge the ſovereignty of the Sultan, who only poſſeſſes in theſe countries a few unimportant towns."

The Paſhas of Ahiſka, of Trebizonde, and Acri, often ſet the Porte at defiance. Near Smyrna the great Agas, or independent chiefs, maintain armies, and often lay that city under contribution. All the inhabitants from Smyrna to Paleſtine are independent, under different lords, and of different religions, and are confidered by the Porte as enemies. In Syria the Sultan[z] virtually poſſeſſes the ports of Latachia (Laodicea), Alexan-

[y] Eton, p. 289.   [z] Eton, p. 292.

dretta

dretta (or Scanderon), the port of Aleppo, Tripoli, Sidon, Jaffa, and a few infignificant places: but the country belongs to the Curds; and the caravans from Scanderon to Aleppo are obliged to go round by Antioch, as they will not fuffer the Turks to pafs through it. In Europe the Morea, Albania, Epirus, and Scutari, are more or lefs in a ftate of rebellion. Bofnea, Croatia, &c. obey the Porte only as long as it fuits them to defend themfelves againft its enemies, in the war with Germany. " Lately we have feen all European Turkey in arms againft the Porte; Adrianople in imminent danger, and even Conftantinople itfelf trembling for its fafety." The advances of Pafwan Oglou become every day more formidable; but the fatal blow will perhaps be ftruck by a power the leaft fufpected by the deluded Mahometans. And when we confider the aftonifhing decreafe in population
throughout

throughout the Empire[a], and the failure of every attempt to revive the antient military spirit of the people[b], since the period

[a] The number of inhabitants in Constantinople is estimated by Mr. Eton at less than 300,000; and he supposes the population of the empire to hold the same proportion with the common calculation. After some inquiry into the causes of this astonishing decrease, he adds, "It is therefore reasonable to conclude, that depopulation could not formerly have made so rapid a progress as at present, and that in a century more, things remaining in their present situation, the Turkish empire will be nearly extinct. It is worthy of remark, that the Curds in the mountains, and other independant tribes who do not mix with the Turks, are exempt from the mortality occasioned by all the calamities, which afflict the countries more immediately subject to the Porte." Eton, p. 270, &c.

[b] Many attempts have been made within the last century, principally by French officers, to renew the antient military spirit of the Turks, and to instruct them in European tactics. Gazi Hassan, the celebrated Pasha, tried, with unlimited power for nineteen years, to inspire his own spirit into

period allotted for the decline of its power; such a combination of circumstances not only justifies the expectation of its fall, upon every principle founded on human experience, but holds out a most striking example of the accuracy of Prophecy, for the contemplation of the present age. The testimony of this unbiassed writer is too valuable to be easily abandoned; and I am much deceived, if the Reader will not see ample confirmation of the system, respecting the three great forms of Antichrist, which the Introductory Chapter offered to his consideration, in the following sketch of the nature and effects of the Mahometan scourge of the *East*—more especially if he will compare the description of this

into the troops; but he found all his efforts ineffectual. The present Sultan, Selim, has attempted to abolish the Janizaries, and introduce the European discipline into the army gradually, by instituting a new corps trained to the musket and bayonet; but this attempt is not likely to succeed to any extent. Eton, chap. iii.

power, with that which has tyrannized over the *West*, for the same purposes of trial and punishment, and with the animated picture of *Jacobinism* in this Author's Address to the Emperor of Russia, which I shall beg leave to subjoin in a note, though it more properly belongs to the subject of the following Chapter[c].

" No

[c] " You are called on, Sire, to crush with the irresistible weight of your armies the enemies of religion, morality, and social order. Peace with them will be more dangerous than war. Their doctrines will have freer course; and their doctrines have done more than their armies. They have subverted the order, and confounded even the names of things. Virtues have the appellations of vices, and vices the appellations of virtues. Can Russia, in all its extended provinces, when every foreign contact will be poison; when every breath, except from the frozen ocean, will be full of miasma, escape the contagion? None will escape but the elder brethren of Jacobinism, the Turks, whose equally monstrous, though less dangerous tyranny, has for so many centuries insulted mankind, trodden under foot the laws of nations, and blasphemed

Chris-

" No defpotifm was ever more profoundly politic than that, which wielding

Chriftianity; who, unprovoked, attacked, conquered, and flaughtered nations without number, murdered their fovereigns, and fpilt every drop of royal blood, maffacred their priefts at the altar, extirpated nobility, plundered the opulent, and bound the wretched remains of the people in fetters of perpetual and hereditary flavery. They alone, till the reign of Jacobinifm had made property a crime, the violation of property a legal refource of government, and the lives and poffeffions of men the right of tyranny; they alone had hitherto confounded the hereditary ranks among mankind; had depreffed genius, learning, and the Chriftian religion, and governed their barbarous empire by flaves and affaffins. Like the Jacobins, they taught Chriftian children to fight againft their fathers, and their fathers' God; they too hold it lawful to murder prifoners in cold blood; they too poffefs a claim to every country in the univerfe, and a facred right to fubject all people to their laws; they too hold all other fovereigns as ufurpers, and dethroning them as the higheft merit. But ftill the Turks have a religion; and though it permits them numberlefs enormities to their own fect, and all enormities

ing at once the temporal and spiritual sword, converted fanaticism itself into an instrument of sovereignty, and united in one person the voice and the arm of the Divinity. In Turkey the judicial and sacerdotal characters are the same. The chief engine of this hierarchy is the *fetva of the Mufti*, a sort of manifesto, which, *like the bulls of the Roman Pontiff*, originating in ecclesiastical power, has been applied to the most important political purposes. In other countries particular reigns, or epochas, have been marked with actions disgraceful to the human species; but *here is a system of wickedness*

mities to others, they acknowledge a God, and many moral duties. Not the contagion of their doctrines was to be feared, but their cruel sword, which once threatened the conquest of the universe, and the extinction of all virtue, dignity, and science in the world: yet was not this first monster so tremendous, in the insolence of his power, as an enemy, as is this second monster, in the insolence of his successes, as a brother." Eton, p. 457.

and

and abomination, transferred from the origin of the nation to its posterity to this very day, confirmed by their religion, and approved by those who call themselves the Priests of God[d]."

"[e] It is scarcely credible, how far the littleness of pride is carried by the Porte, in all their transactions with the Christian Princes. To support their faith, and to extend their empire, are the only law of nations which they acknowledge. Their treaties amount only to a temporary remission of that implacable enmity, with which their religion inspires them against every thing not Mahometan. They consider the most solemn treaties in the light of a *truce*, which they are at liberty to break, whenever they can more effectually serve the cause of Mahomet. In this they

[d] Eton, p. 20, 21.   [e] Eton, p. 106.

are much affifted by the nature of the Arabic language, which they mix with the Turkifh in their public acts, and which, by the various application of its terms, literal and metaphorical, enables them to give whatever interpretation they pleafe to the contract. When they have conquered, they put to death all ages, rank, and fex, except fuch as they make flaves, who are *annually* obliged to ranfom their lives. It has frequently been debated at the Porte, to cut off all the Chriftians in the empire, who will not embrace Mahometanifm; but avarice has in this inftance triumphed over cruelty. Every fpecies of mifery and humiliation attends the Chriftians, who remain firm to their religion, and every honour and advantage is held out to thofe who abandon it."

" ' The effects produced by this mon-

[f] Eton, Preface, p. 5.

ſtrous government in the provinces are ſhocking to behold. We ſeek in vain for a population ſufficient to compoſe thoſe numerous kingdoms and ſtates, which flouriſhed when the Turks uſurped their dominion: we find the country literally a deſert; we find vaſt villages uninhabited, and of many hundreds no traces remain. The empire in its flouriſhing ſtate was a vaſt camp.

" The Fleet goes annually to collect the tribute from Greece and the iſlands in the Archipelago. It is then that the miſerable Greeks[g] moſt feel the weight

[g] Mr. Eton affirms that the character of the Greeks is much ſuperior to what it is uſually repreſented by French writers, in knowledge, ability, ſpirit, and manly courage. They bear the Turkiſh yoke with great impatience, and have long been anxious for aſſiſtance to enable them to ſtrike it off. See his account of their negotiations with the late Empreſs of Ruſſia, chap. ix.

of the iron fceptre that governs them, and all the infults and oppreffion of the vile fatraps of the Tyrant. When a fhip of the fleet arrives in a port, all the people who *can*, fly to the mountains, or into the country. Others fhut themfelves up in their houfes, without daring to ftir out. Every one in the roads and even in the ftreets are plundered by the foldiers and failors of the fhips; and if they are not cut, and wounded with a piftol ball, they efteem themfelves happy. The captains and officers raife contributions for themfelves, and thus the poor Greeks pay another tax to the fleet, which is heavier to thofe on whom it unhappily falls, than that paid to the Sultan; and they are generally prevented from complaining out of fear left the next fhip fhould take revenge."

Such is the government, and fuch are the complicated miferies, under which
the

the East has groaned for many centuries [h]! *The second woe* has been of long duration; but from the view we have first taken of the decline and present state of the Ottoman empire, we are surely authorized to conclude that it *now* draws near its close. It will not however terminate the allotted period of affliction; for when this woe shall be past, "behold, a *third* woe cometh *quickly*"—*while* the *sixth* trumpet *continues* to sound.

In the short account already given of the declining power of the *Papal* Antichrist, we have seen the effects of some

---

[h] When Omar, the Saracen Caliph, took Jerusalem by capitulation in A. D. 637, the Christians were not allowed liberty of worship, but on the most severe and humiliating conditions. See Ockely, Pococke, &c. Omar built a mosque on the site of Solomon's Temple, which remains to this day, walled round at some distance; and it is death for either Jew or Christian to enter the enclosure.

of those vials of wrath which were to be *successively* " poured out upon the men who worship the BEAST and his IMAGE." And the present state of Rome (supposed to be under the influence of the fifth vial) may be considered as a confirmation of the opinion long ago formed by several of the most able Commentators, that the *sixth* vial, which is to be " poured out in the river Euphrates," or the dominion of the *Mahometan* Antichrist, would be contemporary with the *third* woe. The following Chapter will perhaps enable us to conjecture how far the reign of *the* IMAGE, made at the *suggestion*, and acting by the *power*, of the SECOND BEAST, appears to correspond with the THIRD WOE; and how far it seems probable that " the remainder of wrath" will fall with *peculiar* violence upon the votaries of the INFIDEL ANTICHRIST, or, in other words, "upon the worshippers of the IMAGE."

END OF VOL. II.

www.ingramcontent.com/pod-product-compliance
Lightning Source LLC
Chambersburg PA
CBHW030014240426
43672CB00007B/942